Better Homes and Gardens®

food processor cook book

BETTER HOMES AND GARDENS® BOOKS
Editor: Gerald Knox
Art Director: Ernest Shelton
Associate Art Director: Randall Yontz
Copy and Production Editors:
    David Kirchner, Paul S. Kitzke
Food Editor: Doris Eby
Senior Associate Food Editor:
    Sharyl Heiken
Senior Food Editors:
    Sandra Granseth, Elizabeth Woolever
Associate Food Editors:
    Joy Taylor, Patricia Teberg
Recipe Development Editor: Marion Viall
Senior Graphic Designer: Harijs Priekulis
Graphic Designers:
    Faith Berven, Linda Ford,
    Richard Lewis, Sheryl Veenschoten

Food Processor Cook Book
Editor: Diane Nelson
Consultant: Lorene Frohling
Copy and Production Editor: David A. Walsh
Graphic Designer: Neoma Alt West

contents

Cranberry Relish Salad
(see recipe, page 54)

Carrot-Pineapple
Cake (see recipe,
page 90)

Chinese Egg Rolls (see
recipe, page 49)

From appetizer to dessert, a food processor can simplify your kitchen preparations. Use the following primer and chart as reference material when making the recipes.

Skillet Pork Chops and Hot Slaw (see recipe, page 69)

food processing primer

A food processor can be a time-saver when you know how to make the best use of it. But be prepared to spend a little time getting to know your machine and discovering what it can do.

First and foremost, read the owner's manual that came with your processor. It should tell you how to assemble the processor and what specific procedures are recommended.

parts of the machine

Food processors differ from one another in many respects, but they all have certain basic parts in common.

The *motor base* supplies the power and is either direct drive or belt driven, as explained on page 7.

The *work bowl* holds the food for processing. The *cover* for the work bowl has a vertical chute, called the *feed tube*. A *pusher* fits inside the feed tube and is used to guide food into the rotating disks and to reduce spattering when the steel or plastic blade is used.

The work bowl and cover are made of either clear or tinted plastic. Because dark-tinted plastic is hard to see through, you may need to remove the cover in order to judge when the food has been processed to the desired degree.

The sizes and shapes of feed tubes vary. Most, however, are longer than your fingers and are wider at the bottom than at the top. Thus, it is easier sometimes to load foods from the bottom, especially when trying to wedge for a tight fit or when inserting a single food, such as a potato.

When first used, your processor's bowl cover may not turn easily on the bowl. Rub a little cooking oil on the lip of the cover and on the rim of the bowl, then place the cover on the bowl and turn back and forth several times till it moves smoothly.

When processing, try to keep the rim of the work bowl as clean as possible so the cover will always be easy to turn on the bowl.

All processors come with at least three interchangeable cutting tools: the *steel blade* (above, left) which is used for chopping, puréeing, mixing, and kneading; the *slicing disk* (above, second from left); and the *shredding disk* (above, second from right). A *plastic blade* (above, right) comes with some processors; it is used to mix foods when no chopping is required. Symbols such as those above appear at the beginning of each recipe to indicate which blades or disks are to be used.

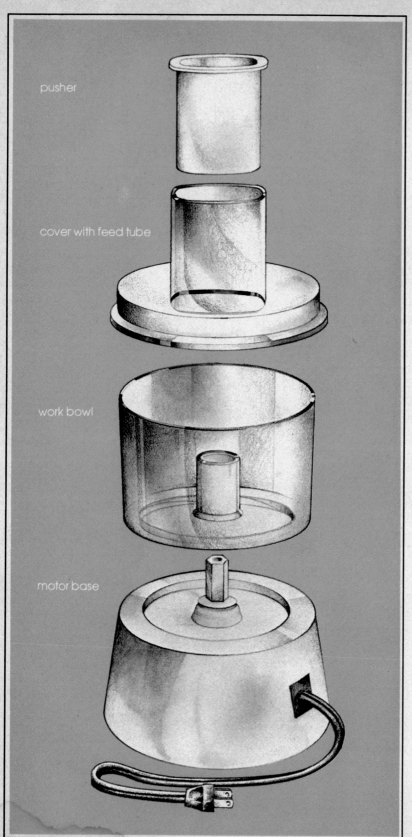

pusher

cover with feed tube

work bowl

motor base

In food processors with a direct-drive motor, the work bowl sits directly atop the motor base, as shown left. In belt-driven units the motor base is either behind or beside the work bowl, as shown below. In most cases the belt-driven processors require a little more counter space than the direct-drive machines, which are higher rather than wider.

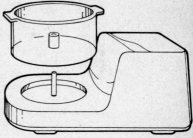

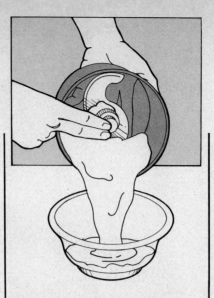

how much to process

Check the owner's manual for the suggested amount to process in your machine. If it isn't given, use a liquid measure to determine how much liquid your work bowl will hold before overflowing at the top or center. Some bowls are marked with a fill line.

The thickness of a food mixture affects the amount that can be processed at one time. Thin mixtures, such as thin soups or beverages are easily spattered, so they must be processed in smaller amounts. Usually 2 cups of liquid is the maximum suggested.

Thick mixtures, such as thick soups or batters, can be processed in larger amounts. Usually 4 cups total mixture is the maximum suggested. This means recipes calling for more than 3 cups of flour must be halved.

Most processors will handle small amounts of food equally as well as they handle large amounts. This is an important feature when processing leftovers or small quantities of food for use in special diets or as baby food.

The actual minimum amount that can be processed varies with each processor. In some models the blade sits closer to the bottom of the bowl, which allows the processing of smaller amounts.

When you are processing larger amounts of foods, it is usually necessary to process in several batches to prevent the work bowl from overflowing.

emptying the work bowl

Some work bowls have a handle that makes them easy to hold while emptying. Most bowls also can be held from the bottom by inserting a finger in the center shaft.

When processing liquids, remove the work bowl from the base but keep the steel or plastic blade in place. This permits the blade to slip down to the bottom of the work bowl and form a seal.

Hold the blade in place with either a spatula or a finger, and tip the bowl to empty the contents, as shown above. This prevents any of the liquid from running down the center shaft. Some processors have a finger hole in the stem of the blade which allows you to hold the blade in the work bowl from the underneath side.

To remove chopped foods, it is usually easiest to remove the blade first. Then you can hold the work bowl with one hand while using a spatula in the other hand to scrape.

If using the slicing or shredding disk, carefully remove the disk before emptying the work bowl.

product uniformity

The processor, like all appliances, has its shortcomings. It does not *perfectly* chop, slice, or shred a food into pieces exactly the same size. If you demand complete uniformity in all these food tasks, then you must do it by hand with a knife. However, most processors perform most of these tasks with near uniformity in a fraction of the time that it takes to do the work by hand.

If the processed food is used in cooked dishes or mixtures, more than likely it will be next to impossible to determine how the food was chopped, shredded, or sliced.

The next eight pages offer specific tips for helping to make the chopped or sliced food as uniform as possible.

processing hot foods

Hot foods can be processed in almost all processors, but be sure to check your owner's manual before doing so. Do not process more than the recommended amount, as described previously. Processed soups, cooked vegetables, and sauces usually can be served immediately after processing. Or, a quick reheating may be necessary.

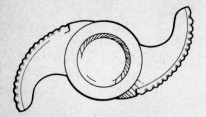

steel blade

The steel blade is the most often used of all the cutting tools. It performs many tasks: chopping, puréeing, mixing, and kneading. Its razor-sharp edges will reduce a bowl of mushrooms to a finely minced mixture in a matter of seconds. The cutting action of the steel blade is amazingly fast, so extreme caution is required to avoid over-processing food.

To use the steel blade, first lock the work bowl on the motor base. Place the steel blade on the motor shaft, making certain the blade is all the way down on the shaft. Cover and process.

chopping basics

A fairly dry work bowl is needed for most chopping tasks. Some foods such as parsley, nuts, breads, and crackers, require a thoroughly dry bowl. If you think that there is moisture in the work bowl, insert the steel blade in the empty work bowl and place the cover on it. Then start and stop the machine. Use a paper towel to carefully wipe away any moisture that appears on the side of the bowl. Repeat till the bowl stays dry after the machine has been run empty for a few seconds.

When chopping, never attempt to process more than 2 cups of food at one time. For meat, chop only ½ pound or 1 cup meat cubes at a time before emptying the work bowl. By limiting the amount of food chopped at once, you will get a more uniform chop.

Another way to help achieve a uniform chop is to try to have the food in approximately the same size pieces. If it is a combination of large and small pieces, the final chop will be a mixture of coarsely and finely chopped food. The pieces of food also should be distributed evenly in the work bowl, as shown below.

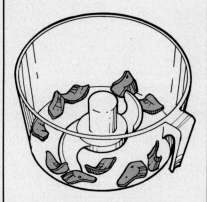

A very commonly used method for chopping is to place the food in the work bowl, and then quickly start and stop the processor by turning it on and off.

This on/off method usually is used to process soft or medium-firm foods, such as apples, onions, and mushrooms. The quick starting-and-stopping action gives you better control over the coarseness or fineness of the chop because you can easily check the food each time you stop the processor. Also, this method permits the larger pieces in the work bowl to fall away from the sides of the bowl into the path of the blade, resulting in a more uniform chop. If necessary, use a spatula to scrape down the sides of the work bowl when the machine is stopped.

The on/off method involves very quick action. To better understand just how fast this method is, place the cover on the empty work bowl and practice starting and stopping your machine several times in quick succession. The trick is to turn off the machine immediately after you have turned it on.

Some processors are equipped with a pulse-action button that turns the machine on and off quickly as you touch and release the button.

As you become more experienced with the quick cutting action of the blade, you may not need to start and stop the machine quite as frequently as in the beginning.

A second, although less frequently used, method of chopping involves adding food to the work bowl through the feed tube while the machine is running. This is used usually with firm foods, such as root vegetables and hard cheeses. One disadvantage of this method is that food added first may become overprocessed.

This method is designed to prevent a piece of food from becoming wedged between the bowl and steel blade, thus stalling the processor. Should a piece of food become wedged, simply disconnect the machine, remove the cover, and carefully remove the trapped food. If it is necessary to remove the steel blade in order to free the food, make certain the blade is properly reinserted in the work bowl before resuming processing.

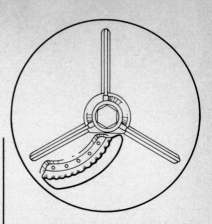

puréeing basics

To purée in the processor, place the steel blade in the work bowl, then add the food. Place the cover on the work bowl; turn the machine on and let run till the food is smooth. Stop the machine occasionally to scrape the bowl's sides.

When puréeing foods cooked in liquids, such as soups, purée the strained solids first, then return to the cooking broth. It is not necessary to add liquid to the work bowl when puréeing; in fact, smoother purée results when cooked foods are processed alone. Remember not to process more than 2 cups at a time.

mixing basics

Although the processor is not an electric mixer, it can fill some of the same functions in preparing recipes.

In some cases, all ingredients are added to the work bowl at once and processed together.

In other recipes, as for cookies and quick breads, the sugar and butter are creamed before the flour and seasonings are added.

Remember, there's no need to bring butter, shortening, or cream cheese to room temperature before processing, as the processor will easily cream them when they're cold. Simply quarter or cube them before adding to work bowl.

kneading doughs

The steel blade is also efficient in kneading bread and pastry doughs. For, those who are hesitant about breadmaking, the processor offers a quick method for making a handsome loaf of bread. However, some processors will not handle heavy doughs, so be sure to follow the manufacturer's recommendations for your machine.

When working with any dough in the processor, never use more than 3 cups of flour. Also, to avoid a tough product, never process the dough more than 60 seconds. If the motor begins to slow down, immediately stop the machine and add a little more flour (1 to 2 tablespoons is usually enough) to the work bowl. This should free the dough from the blades and the motor should return to normal speed.

beating and whipping

The processor cannot replace your rotary beater or electric mixer for beating egg whites or whipping cream. It is not designed to incorporate air into the food it processes; instead it breaks the air bubbles as they form. Thus, the final volume when processing these foods is considerably less than when they are beaten or whipped in the conventional way.

It is possible, however, to whip cream when volume is not so important, such as for dessert toppings. Watch carefully, because the processing can quickly turn the cream into butter.

slicing disk

The slicing disk is an efficient tool for slicing soft foods as well as firm ones. Your satisfaction with the sliced product will depend on the particular processor you use. Some slice strawberries as well as they do carrots; others work satisfactorily only on the firmer foods. Also, most machines offer only one thickness of slice, which may be thinner than the thickness usually obtained when sliced by hand.

The slicing disk on some processors successfully slices raw and cooked meat as well as hard sausages (remove casing before slicing). However, be sure to check manufacturer's recommendations for your machine before slicing meat because it may cause serious damage to a processor not designed for this purpose.

To slice, lock the work bowl on the motor base, then place the slicing disk on the motor shaft in the bowl. Make certain the disk is all the way down on the shaft. Place the cover on the work bowl; note that the cutting edge of the disk is resting directly below the cover of the bowl. Place the food in the feed tube, trimming the food if necessary to fit. Leave at least an inch of space at the top of the feed tube when filling. Slice, using the pusher to guide the food through the blade. The space left at the top of the feed tube gives the pusher more leverage, making it more useful as a guiding tool.

The thickness of the slices varies with the pressure exerted by the pusher. Heavy pressure produces thicker slices, and light pressure gives thinner slices. In general, use light-to-medium pressure for soft-textured foods; medium-to-firm pressure for firm-textured foods. Never use fingers or any utensil except the pusher to guide the food into the cutting disk.

Foods often require trimming or halving before they will fit in the feed tube. However, before trimming food that appears too large for the feed tube, try to insert it from the bottom of the tube. The feed tube is designed so that it is slightly larger at the base than at the top.

When uniform slices are not important, merely drop the food into the feed tube, as shown below. If this method is used for slicing small foods, such as mushrooms, olives, and strawberries, the slices will be uniform in thickness. However, the slices will be angled as well as straight. Food is sliced very quickly in this manner, and the slices, although not perfect in appearance, are readily acceptable for use in casseroles, sauces, cooked dishes, and frozen desserts.

When you need nearly perfect slices, arrange the food in the feed tube in layers, as shown above. It is sometimes helpful to cut a flat edge on the side of the food that rests on the slicing disk. Fit the food snugly in the tube to prevent the force of the whirling disk from flipping the pieces of food crosswise before slicing.

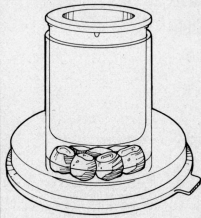

When slicing foods for garnishes, you will usually have better results if you slice only one layer of food at a time, as shown above. This is much more time-consuming but produces more nearly perfect slices. Because the feed tube is longer than your fingers, use small tongs, long-handled tweezers, or the tip of a knife to arrange the food in the tube so it rests on the disk.

When slicing longer foods, such as carrots, bananas, or pickles, cut the food in equal lengths about 1 inch shorter than the feed tube. Wedge vertically in feed tube making a snug fit, as shown below. The wedging prevents the food from falling over in the feed tube, which would result in angled slices.

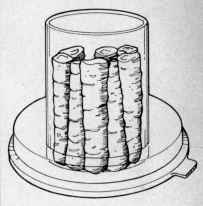

Medium- to large-size foods, such as onions and cucumbers, must be halved vertically before being placed in the feed tube. However, you often can wedge two small halves in the tube together by placing the two cut surfaces face to face with edges overlapping, as shown below.

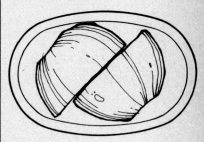

When slicing a fruit or vegetable that has peel on one side only, such as a halved green pepper or apple, position the food in the tube so the peel faces the center of the work bowl. This way the cutting edge of the disk will come in contact with the peel first. If the food is placed with the peel facing out, some machines may tend to skin off the peel rather than cut through it.

It is not uncommon for a small amount of food to remain atop the slicing disk after having been sliced. However, the waste is minimal because the succeeding food placed in the tube usually forces the food that remained atop the disk through the blade.

If the work bowl is marked with a fill line, empty the bowl when the food reaches this level. For work bowls without such markings, empty the food when the bowl is almost full.

julienne basics

Julienne or matchstick cuts are ideal for salads, soups, and shoestring potatoes. They are made by slicing slices. First slice the food as just described. Empty the bowl and reinsert the slicing disk. Reassemble the cut food slices and place them in the feed tube.

Some foods such as sliced beets are wet enough to stick together when reassembled and can be carefully dropped into the feed tube from the top.

Other foods, however, may need to be inserted from the bottom. Turn the cover of the work bowl on its side and pull the pusher out of the feed tube about 2 inches. Insert the cut slices parallel to the sides of the feed tube, as shown below. Wedge in the last slice for a snug fit. Carefully replace the cover on the work bowl and slice.

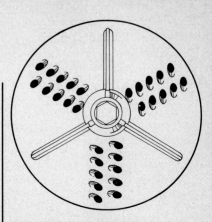

shredding disk

Shredding in the processor not only is fast and easy but eliminates nicks and cuts on fingers, as you may get from hand shredders. It often is more convenient to shred some foods in quantity, then wrap into small amounts and refrigerate or freeze for later use.

Metal shavings sometimes remain on the cutting edges of the shredding disk as it comes from the manufacturer. To remove these stray particles, shred a firm food, such as a carrot, turnip, or potato and then discard it. Thoroughly wash the disk and work bowl, and they will be ready to use.

The shred produced in the processor can be very fine. In some recipes you may prefer to chop the food with the steel blade rather than to shred it. Preparing cabbage for coleslaw is an example of this.

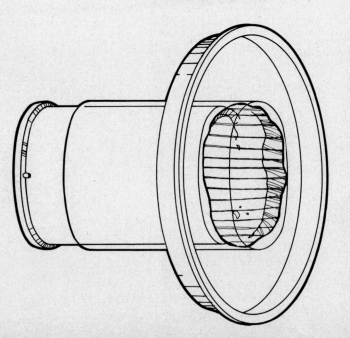

To shred, lock the work bowl on the motor base. Place the shredding disk on the motor shaft in the bowl. Make certain the disk is all the way down on the shaft. Place the cover on the work bowl; note that the cutting edge of the disk is directly below the cover. Halve or trim the food to fit in the feed tube, if necessary. Remember it's sometimes easier to insert food from the bottom, but wedge it tightly so it won't fall out when placed over the disk. Remember, also, to leave at least an inch of space at the top of the feed tube to allow for the pusher.

Place the food in the feed tube and shred, using the pusher to guide the food through the disk. As with slicing, use light-to-medium pressure for soft-textured foods and medium-to-firm pressure for firm-textured foods. Always follow your owner's manual for shredding. Some foods may become mushy or, as in the case of soft cheese, the heat generated by the rapid turning of the disk may warm the cheese to the extent that it may either form little balls atop the disk or become gummy.

Depending on how food is placed in the feed tube, the shreds may be either short or long. For short shreds, wedge the food upright in the feed tube. For longer shreds, drop the food horizontally into the feed tube.

If the work bowl is marked with a fill line, empty the bowl when the food reaches this level. For bowls without such markings, empty the bowl when it is almost full.

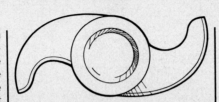

plastic blade

The plastic blade is a standard tool with some processors. Its use is limited to mixing or blending ingredients since it does not have a cutting edge.

Use the plastic blade for mixing foods that require no chopping, such as dips, sauces, and salad dressings. You also can use it for mixing thin batters, such as for crepes. However, the steel blade works equally well in performing all of the tasks assigned to the plastic blade, so its use will depend more upon personal preference.

To use the plastic blade, lock the work bowl on the motor base. Place the plastic blade on the motor shaft, making certain it is all the way down on the shaft. Add the ingredients to the bowl and process till well blended, stopping as needed to scrape down the sides of the bowl. Leave the blade in place and remove work bowl to empty the processed food.

recipe & meal preparation

Use the processor to shortcut preparation tasks in individual recipes as well as in total meal preparation. Learn to think through the total menu, looking for ways to consolidate preparations before starting to work. For example, if you need chopped onion for a meat loaf and for a vegetable casserole, process enough onion for both foods at the same time.

To eliminate excess bowl washing, process dry foods before wet ones, even though the dry ones may not be needed till last.

If several foods require chopping for a recipe, it is often possible to process together similar textured foods, such as apples and pears. Remember not to process more than the recommended amount at one time.

Foods that are not similar in texture must be processed separately. You will not get a satisfactory chop if you attempt to chop green pepper, which is watery, with carrots, which are firm. If you have any doubt as to whether you can satisfactorily chop two foods together, it is better to chop them separately.

One way to shortcut recipe preparation is to process foods in quantity and store them in the refrigerator or freezer for later use. A few examples are shredded cheese, shredded coconut, chopped onion, chopped nuts, chopped parsley, and soft and dry bread crumbs. These commonly used foods are convenient to have already prepared and ready to use.

With a little practice, you will quickly learn how to mentally rearrange the ingredients in your favorite recipes for use in the processor. For guidelines and example recipes, see page 36.

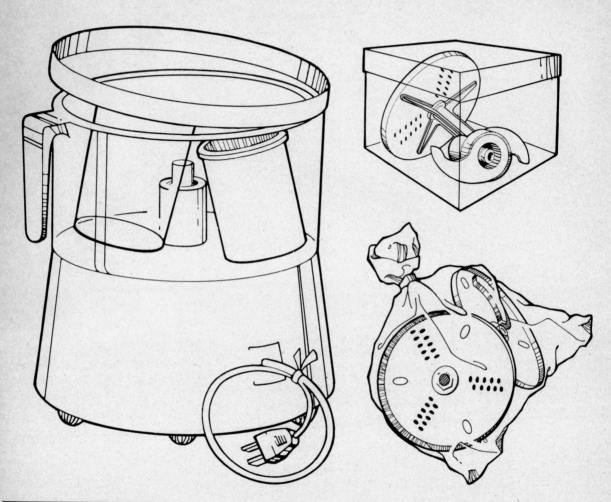

storing your processor

A food processor can be an important aid to meal preparation once you master the basic techniques of its use and train yourself to look for tasks it can simplify in the kitchen. But, it is useful only if it's easily accessible. Try to store it in a convenient location where it's easy to get at everyday.

When storing your processor, never leave the work bowl atop the motor base with the cover turned to the on position. Instead, store the cover in the off position atop the work bowl, or invert the cover and place it in the open bowl, as shown above. Leaving the cover in the on position may eventually damage the spring mechanism in the motor start switch on some processors.

It is also a good idea to store the processor with the pusher out of the feed tube; this allows air to circulate through the work bowl, not only drying it, but also eliminating odors.

Store cutting tools either in specially designed racks for processor blades or in a separate location away from other often used kitchen utensils. Cut fingers are inevitable if you store processor tools in frequently opened drawers. It is important also to store processor blades out of the reach of small children. It may be easiest to keep all the blades and disks in a heavy plastic bag or box.

cleaning your processor

The key to an easy cleanup is to rinse the parts immediately after using. There's no need to thoroughly dry the work bowl and its parts unless further processing requires a dry bowl. Promptly wipe up any spills on the motor base or cord using a clean, damp cloth.

Never soak the steel blade or cutting disks in a dishpan of soapy water. You might forget they are there, reach into the water and cut your fingers on them.

A vegetable brush or other dishwashing brush with a long handle makes cleaning the blades and disks not only easier but safer. It eliminates the possibility of cut fingers and ensures that minute food particles are removed from the sharp cutting tools.

A pipe cleaner or small round brush, such as the kind you use to clean coffeepot stems, is ideal for removing any food that might become trapped in the underneath side of the stem of the cutting tools.

Parts of some processors are dishwasherproof. Be certain to follow manufacturer's recommendations before placing any parts in the dishwasher.

safety precautions

1. All family members who will be using the processor should carefully read and follow all instructions that accompany the machine before operating it.

2. The cutting edges of the disks and the steel blade are very sharp and must be handled carefully.

3. Disconnect the processor before changing blades or disks, before cleaning, and when not in use.

4. Always lock the work bowl on the motor base before inserting the blade or disk.

5. Make certain the cutting tool is all the way down on the motor shaft before starting to process. Serious damage to the processor could result if the cutting tool is not properly in place.

6. Always use the pusher for feeding food through the feed tube; never use other utensils or your fingers.

7. Make certain the blade or disk has come to a complete stop before removing the cover of the work bowl.

8. Store blades and disks in a safe place out of the reach of small children.

9. Keep hands, utensils, and spatulas away from moving blades or disks to prevent personal injury or damage to the processor.

10. Do not let the cord of the processor hang over the countertop or touch hot surfaces.

11. Never immerse the processor base in water or other liquid.

12. Most processors have an automatic circuit breaker that shuts off the motor when it overheats. Follow manufacturer's directions for restarting.

13. If your processor doesn't have an automatic circuit breaker, be alert for signs of overheating, especially when processing thick or heavy batters, or when using the processor for long periods of time. Stop immediately if the motor sounds overworked or if the motor base feels warm.

food processing chart

The next 19 pages offer how-to-do-it directions and tips for processing a variety of foods. Photographs show how to load the feed tube and how the food will appear after being processed. All are arranged alphabetically within categories. Check here before processing a food you haven't done before.

The food processor is a speed machine that can quickly turn whole foods into slices, shreds, chopped pieces, or puréed mixtures. A major factor to the successful use of the machine is realizing just how fast it works and learning to stop before food is overprocessed.

The acceptability of the sliced, shredded, chopped, or puréed food that you get from your processor will depend on the particular processor used and also on your planned use for the processed food.

As a general rule, foods sliced, shredded, or chopped in the processor are nearly always acceptable for use in cooked products. But for garnishing or other uses where appearance is especially important, you probably will obtain more satisfactory results from cutting by hand.

For the most even slices, fit the food as tightly as possible into the feed tube. This prevents pieces from leaning to one side, giving diagonal slices. For the tightest fit, you may want to fill the feed tube from the bottom, since it is usually slightly larger than the top. Be careful when placing the cover over the slicing disk so as not to scrape your hand or fingers across it.

When slicing foods with peels, such as apples and green peppers, some machines may tend to skin off the peel rather than cut through it. If you have trouble with this, place the piece of food into the feed tube so that the peel faces the center of the work bowl. This way the blade of the slicing disk will hit the side with the peel first and be more likely to cut through it.

For both slicing and shredding, you will see directions written to cut the food to be processed into lengths 1 inch shorter than the feed tube, or to fill the tube within 1 inch of the top. This is to leave leverage room at the top for the pusher to be partially inserted. This way all foods will be forced into the disk with the same amount of pressure, thus giving a more uniform product.

When chopping hard foods, such as nuts, chilled chocolate, carrots, and hard cheese, be prepared for loud noise as the pieces are thrown against the sides of the work bowl.

Where applicable in this chart, yields have been included along with the directions for processing. Remember that these are approximate and may not be exactly the same as the results you get.

dairy products

cheese

crumbled (blue)
Place steel blade in work bowl. Cut well-chilled cheese into 1-inch pieces; place up to 1 cup in work bowl. Process with on/off turns. Sprinkle on salads or use in salad dressings, dips, and cheese balls.
4 ounces = 1 cup

cheese (very hard)

grated (parmesan, romano)
Place steel blade in work bowl. Cut cheese into 1-inch pieces; place up to 1 cup pieces in work bowl. Process to desired fineness. Sprinkle over soups and vegetables or use in cooking.
4 ounces = 1 cup

cheese (firm or processed)

shredded (cheddar, American, Swiss, and mozzarella)
Place shredding disk in work bowl. Trim well-chilled cheese to fit feed tube (or fold purchased sliced cheese in half); place in feed tube. Use medium-to-firm pressure with pusher for firm cheeses; use light-to-medium pressure for processed cheeses. Use for cooking or add to salads and sandwich fillings. If desired, wrap tightly in moisture-vaporproof material or pack in freezer containers. Freeze up to 6 months.
4 ounces = 1 cup

cottage cheese

puréed
Place steel blade in work bowl; add 1½ to 2 cups cottage cheese. Process just till smooth, occasionally stopping machine to scrape down sides of bowl. Use in dips and salad dressings.

cream cheese

creamed
Cream cheese does not have to be brought to room temperature before processing. Place steel blade in work bowl. Cut cream cheese into quarters or cubes; add to work bowl. Process till smooth. Most machines will handle up to three 8-ounce packages at one time. If your machine balks, do only one or two packages at a time. Use in cooking and baking.

cream

whipped to make butter
Place steel blade in work bowl; pour 2 cups whipping cream into bowl. Process till thickened. With machine running, add ¼ cup cold water through feed tube; continue processing till solids separate out. Drain thoroughly; pat butter dry with paper toweling. Use as spread and for cooking and baking.

whipped for topping
Place steel blade in work bowl; add ¼ to 2 cups whipping cream. Process just till soft peaks form (about 30 seconds for 1 cup). Sweeten with a little sugar, if desired. Cream whipped in the processor will not have as much volume as cream whipped in an electric mixer. Spoon over desserts.

fruits

apples

sliced
Place slicing disk in work bowl. Peel apples, if desired; quarter and core. Stack apple quarters horizontally on edge in feed tube as shown in top photo, above. Slice, using medium pressure with pusher. Use in salads or pies and other baked desserts.
1 medium = ¾ to 1 cup sliced

chopped
Place steel blade in work bowl. Peel apples, if desired; core. Cut into 1-inch pieces; place up to 2 cups pieces in work bowl. Process with on/off turns till chopped to desired size. Use in relishes, salads, fillings, and baked goods.
1 medium = ¾ to 1 cup chopped

apricots

sliced
Place slicing disk in work bowl. Halve apricots; pit. Place apricot halves, cut side down (or wedge halves together vertically) in feed tube. Slice, using light pressure with pusher. Use in fruit cups and desserts.

avocados

mashed
Place steel blade in work bowl. Quarter, seed, and peel avocados; place in work bowl. Process till smooth, stopping to scrape down sides of work bowl, as needed. Use in dips, spreads, and sauces.

sliced
The acceptability of sliced avocados depends on the processor. With some machines the resultant slices may be too thin to be usable.
Insert slicing disk. Halve, seed, and peel avocados. Place, vertically, in feed tube (for large avocados, it may be easier to insert the avocado half, small end first, into the feed tube from the bottom). Slice avocados, using light pressure with pusher. Use in salads.

bananas

sliced
Place slicing disk in work bowl. Peel bananas; halve crosswise. Place bananas, cut side down, in feed tube, as shown above. Slice, using light pressure with pusher (slices will be very thin). Use in fruit salads and pies or other desserts.

mashed
Place steel blade in work bowl. Peel bananas (ripe ones mash best); cut into 1-inch pieces. Place up to 1 cup pieces in work bowl. Process till smooth, stopping to scrape down sides of work bowl as needed. Use in baking.
1 medium (about 6 inches) = ⅓ cup mashed banana

berries

puréed
Use fresh or thawed frozen strawberries, raspberries, or blueberries. Place steel blade in work bowl; add up to 2 cups of the fruit. Process till smooth. Strain, if desired, to remove seeds. Use in beverages and frozen desserts.

candied fruit

chopped
Place steel blade in work bowl. Add up to 1 cup candied fruit. Add ½ cup all-purpose flour or sugar per cup fruit to prevent the blade from gumming up. Process with on/off turns till chopped to desired size. Use in baked goods; remember to subtract the amount of flour or sugar used in chopping from the amount needed in recipe.

cantaloupe

puréed
Place steel blade in work bowl. Halve cantaloupe and discard seeds; scoop out pulp. Add up to 2 cups pulp to work bowl; process till smooth. Use in beverages and frozen desserts or salads.

cherries

chopped
Place steel blade in work bowl. Remove stems and pits from cherries. Place up to 1 cup cherries in work bowl. Process with on/off turns till chopped to desired size. Use in baking, fillings, and jams.

citrus fruit

sliced
Insert slicing disk in work bowl. Halve or quarter fruit lengthwise and trim ends. Wedge halves or quarters vertically in feed tube. Slice, using firm pressure with pusher; slices will be irregular. (Some processors may spray juice during slicing.) Use as garnish or float slices in punch bowl.

grated peel
Place steel blade in work bowl. Use vegetable peeler to cut strips of outer portion of peel from lemons, limes, or oranges. Cut peel into 1-inch pieces. Add to work bowl along with sugar or nuts from recipe (peel will not process very well by itself). Process till desired fineness. Use in baking and for salads and desserts.
1 inch strip peel = ⅛ teaspoon grated peel

juiced
Place steel blade in work bowl. Peel lemons, limes, or oranges removing all of white membrane. Halve fruit and remove seeds. Place up to 4 pieces of halved fruit in work bowl; process till finely chopped. Strain.
1 medium lemon = 3 tablespoons
1 medium lime = 2 tablespoons
1 medium orange = ¼ to ⅓ cup

cranberries

sliced
Place slicing disk in work bowl. Pour fresh or thawed frozen cranberries into feed tube to within 1 inch of top. Slice, using light pressure with pusher. Use in relishes, salads, fillings, and quick breads.
1 cup (4 ounces) = ¾ to 1 cup

chopped
Place steel blade in work bowl. Add up to 1 cup fresh or thawed frozen cranberries. Process with on/off turns till chopped to desired size, stopping to scrape down sides of work bowl as needed. Chopped cranberries will be similar in appearance to sliced cranberries, as shown above. Use in relishes, salads, fillings, and quick breads.
1 cup (4 ounces) = ¾ to 1 cup

fruits continued

dried fruit

chopped
Place steel blade in work bowl. Add up to 1 cup dried fruit. Add ¼ cup all-purpose flour or sugar per cup of fruit to prevent the blade from gumming up. Process with on/off turns till chopped to desired size. Use in fillings and in baking, but remember to subtract the amount of flour or sugar used in chopping from the amount needed in the recipe.

nectarines

sliced
Place slicing disk in work bowl. Halve nectarines; pit. Peel, if desired. Place nectarine halves vertically in feed tube. Slice, using light pressure with pusher. Use in fresh fruit cups or desserts.

peaches

sliced
Place slicing disk in work bowl. Halve and pit peaches; peel if desired. Place peach halves vertically in feed tube. Slice, using light pressure with pusher. Use in fruit cups, pies, or other desserts.
1 large (6 ounces) = 1 cup sliced

chopped
Processing tends to mash ripe peaches rather than chop them. Firm peaches may give an acceptable product; follow directions for *pears, chopped.*

pears

sliced
Place slicing disk in work bowl. Peel pears, if desired; quarter and core. For pear-shaped slices, place small pears horizontally in feed tube, as shown in top photo, above. (Cut large pears in half and place vertically in feed tube.) Slice, using light pressure with pusher. Use in fruit cup, pies, and other desserts.
1 medium = ⅔ to ¾ cups sliced

chopped
Place steel blade in work bowl. Peel pears, if desired; core. Cut into 1-inch pieces; place up to 1 cup pieces in work bowl. Process with on/off turns till chopped to desired size. Use in relishes, jams, fillings, and baked foods.
1 medium = ⅔ to ¾ cup chopped

pineapple

sliced
Place slicing disk in work bowl. Trim ends from pineapple. Peel; remove eyes and core. Cut pineapple into wedges about 1 inch shorter than height of feed tube, as shown in top photo, above. Slice using medium pressure with pusher. Use in fruit cups and salads.
1 3- to 4-pound pineapple = 3 cups sliced

pineapple

chopped
Place steel blade in work bowl. Trim ends from pineapple. Peel; remove eyes and core. Cut pineapple into 1-inch pieces; place up to 1 cup pieces in work bowl. Process with on/off turns till chopped to desired size. Use in fruit cups, sauces, jams, and desserts.
1 3- to 4-pound pineapple = 3 cups chopped

plums

sliced
Place slicing disk in work bowl. Halve plums; pit. Place plum halves, cut side down (or wedge halves together vertically), in feed tube. Slice, using light pressure with pusher. Use in salads and desserts.

chopped
Place steel blade in work bowl. Halve plums; place up to 1 cup pieces in work bowl. Process with on/off turns till chopped to desired size. Use in quick breads, desserts, and jams.

raspberries

puréed
See *berries, puréed,* page 18.

rhubarb

sliced
Place slicing disk in work bowl. Remove strings from rhubarb, if desired. Cut rhubarb into equal lengths about 1 inch shorter than height of feed tube. Place in feed tube, wedging in last piece for a tight fit (keeps pieces straight vertically). Slice, using medium pressure with pusher. (Slices will be thin.) Use in pies, sauces, desserts, and quick breads.
8 ounces = 2 cups sliced

strawberries

sliced
Place slicing disk in work bowl. Select firm ripe berries; hull. Arrange berries horizontally in feed tube. Slice, using light pressure with pusher. Use in pies, desserts, sauces, and jams.
2 cups = 1½ cups sliced

puréed
See *berries, puréed,* page 18.

meat, fish, poultry, & eggs

bacon

crumbled
Place steel blade in work bowl. Cook bacon till crisp; drain. Place up to 6 strips cooked bacon in work bowl. Process with on/off turns till crumbled. Use in casseroles, crumb toppings, and salads.

beef (uncooked)

sliced
Place slicing disk in work bowl. Remove bone, gristle, and excess fat from meat; trim meat to fit feed tube, as shown above. Remember to insert from bottom to avoid excess trimming. Partially freeze meat for most uniform slices. Slice, using firm pressure with pusher. Use in stir-fry cooking.

beef (uncooked)

chopped
Place steel blade in work bowl. Remove bone, gristle, and excess fat from meat. Fat adds flavor and juiciness, so leave some on meat unless chopped meat is to be used for Steak Tartare (see recipe, page 48) or for a special diet where lean meat is necessary. Cut meat into 1-inch pieces; place up to 1 cup meat pieces in work bowl. Process with on/off turns till chopped to desired size. A medium to medium-fine chop, as shown above, is similar to purchased ground beef. Use in all recipes calling for ground beef.
1 pound lean boneless beef = 1 pound chopped

beef (cooked)

chopped
Place steel blade in work bowl. Remove bone, gristle, and excess fat from meat; cut meat into 1-inch pieces. Place up to 1 cup meat pieces in work bowl. Process with on/off turns till chopped to desired size. Use for sandwich fillings, meat pies, casseroles, and hash.
1 pound cooked beef = 3 cups chopped

chicken (uncooked)

sliced
Place slicing disk in work bowl. Bone and skin whole chicken breasts. Roll or fold in half and fit in feed tube (use two, if small), as shown above. Insert from bottom for easiest fitting. Slice, using medium pressure with pusher. Use for stir-fry cooking.

chicken (cooked)

chopped
Place steel blade in work bowl. Bone and skin cooked chicken; cut into 1-inch pieces. Place up to 1 cup chicken pieces in work bowl. Process with on/off turns till chopped to desired size. Use in casseroles and sandwich fillings.
1 pound cooked chicken = 3 cups chopped

eggs (hard-cooked)

chopped
Place steel blade in work bowl. Halve hard-cooked eggs; place up to 1 cup halves in work bowl. Process with on/off turns till chopped to desired size, as shown above. Use in sandwich fillings or sprinkle over tossed salads or vegetables.

fish (uncooked)

puréed
Place steel blade in work bowl. Remove skin and bones from fish; cut fish into 1-inch pieces. Place up to 1 cup pieces in work bowl. Process till mixture is smooth, stopping to scrape down sides of work bowl as needed. Use in mousses and quenelles.

fish (canned)

puréed
Place steel blade in work bowl. Drain canned fish; remove skin, bones, and cartilage, if desired. Place up to 1 cup fish in work bowl. Process till mixture is smooth, stopping to scrape down sides of work bowl as needed. Use in dips and spreads.

ham (fully cooked)

chopped
Place steel blade in work bowl. Remove bone and fat from ham; cut ham into 1-inch pieces. Place up to 1 cup ham pieces in work bowl. Process with on/off turns till chopped to desired size. Use in sandwich fillings and spreads.
1 pound ham = 3 cups chopped

lamb (uncooked)

chopped
Place steel blade in work bowl. Remove bone, gristle, and excess fat from meat. Fat adds flavor and juiciness, so leave some on meat. Cut lamb into 1-inch pieces; place up to 1 cup pieces in work bowl. Process with on/off turns till chopped to desired size; see illustration for *beef (uncooked), chopped*. Use in all recipes calling for ground lamb.
1 pound lean boneless lamb = 1 pound chopped

luncheon meats

julienne
Place slicing disk in work bowl. Using an 8-ounce package of square-shaped sliced luncheon meat (round slices do not work as well), carefully fold stacked slices in half. Place in feed tube, as shown above. Slice, using light pressure with pusher. Use in salads or sandwich fillings.

meat, fish, poultry, & eggs continued

pepperoni

sliced
Place slicing disk in work bowl. Remove casing from pepperoni. Cut pepperoni into equal lengths about 1-inch shorter than height of feed tube; arrange vertically in feed tube for compact fit. Slice, using medium to firm pressure with pusher. Use in sandwiches, pizza, salads, and sauces.

chopped
Place steel blade in work bowl. Remove casing from pepperoni; cut pepperoni into ½-inch pieces. Start machine; drop pepperoni pieces through feed tube. Process till chopped to desired size. Use in main dishes.

pork (uncooked)

sliced
Place slicing disk in work bowl. Remove bone, gristle, and excess fat from meat. Trim meat to fit feed tube, referring to *beef (uncooked), sliced,* page 22. Partially freeze meat for most uniform slices. Place pork in feed tube (insert from bottom for easiest fit). Slice, using firm pressure with pusher. Use in stir-fry cooking.

pork (uncooked)

chopped
Place steel blade in work bowl. Remove bone, gristle, and excess fat from pork. Fat adds flavor and juiciness, so leave some on meat unless chopped meat is for special diet. Cut meat into 1-inch pieces; place up to 1 cup pork pieces in work bowl. Process with on/off turns till chopped to desired size; see illustration for *beef (uncooked), chopped,* page 22. Use in all recipes calling for ground pork.
1 pound lean boneless pork = 1 pound chopped

pork (cooked)

chopped
Place steel blade in work bowl. Remove bone, gristle, and fat from cooked pork; cut meat into 1-inch pieces. Place up to 1 cup pork pieces in work bowl. Process with on/off turns till chopped to desired size. Use in sandwich fillings, meat pies, and casseroles.
1 pound cooked pork = 3 cups chopped

sausage (hard)

sliced
See *pepperoni, sliced.*
chopped
See *pepperoni, chopped.*

seafood (cooked)

chopped
Place steel blade in work bowl. Shell cooked seafood; devein, if using shrimp. Cut seafood into 1-inch pieces; place up to 1 cup in work bowl. Process with on/off turns till chopped to desired size. Use in dips, spreads, and sauces.

turkey (uncooked)

chopped
Place steel blade in work bowl. Thaw a frozen turkey drumstick. Cut meat from bones; discard bones. Cut meat into 1-inch pieces. Place up to 1 cup pieces in work bowl. Process with on/off turns till chopped to desired size; see illustration for *beef (uncooked), chopped,* page 22. Use in all recipes calling for ground turkey.

turkey (cooked)

chopped
Place steel blade in work bowl. Bone and skin cooked turkey. Cut meat into 1-inch pieces. Place up to 1 cup pieces in work bowl. Process with on/off turns till chopped to desired size. Use in casseroles, sandwich fillings, and spreads.
1 pound cooked turkey = 3 cups chopped

veal (uncooked)

chopped
Place steel blade in work bowl. Remove bone, gristle, and excess fat from veal. Cut veal into 1-inch pieces. Place up to 1 cup meat pieces in work bowl. Process with on/off turns till chopped to desired size; see illustration for *beef (uncooked), chopped,* page 22. Use in all recipes calling for ground veal.

veal (cooked)

chopped
See *beef (cooked), chopped,* page 22.

vegetables

beans (green)

french-cut

Place slicing disk in work bowl. Remove ends and strings from beans. Cut beans into lengths to fit width of feed tube. Place beans horizontally in feed tube to within 1 inch of top, as shown above. Slice, using medium pressure with pusher. Cook and serve, or use in casseroles, salads, and soups.
6 ounces = 1⅓ cups french-cut

beets

sliced

Select small to medium beets. For uncooked beets, peel. For cooked beets, cut off all but 1 inch of stems and roots. In covered pan cook beets in boiling salted water for 35 to 50 minutes or till tender. Cool slightly; slip off skins. Place slicing disk in work bowl. Stack uncooked or cooked beets upright in feed tube (halve large ones vertically, if necessary, to fit tube.) Slice, using light pressure with pusher. Add uncooked beets to soups; serve cooked beets alone or use in salads and casseroles.
¾ to 1 pound beets with tops = 1⅓ cups sliced

beets

julienne

Slice beets as directed below left, remove. Reinsert slicing disk. Put beet slices in feed tube, as shown above, slice. Add uncooked beets to soups; serve cooked beets alone or use in salads and relishes.
¾ to 1 pound beets with tops = 1⅓ cups julienne strips

cabbage

shredded

Insert shredding disk. Core and cut cabbage into wedges to fit feed tube; shred, (texture will be very fine). Use in salads and relishes.
1 1-pound head cabbage = 4 to 5 cups shredded

cabbage

sliced

Place slicing disk in work bowl. Core cabbage; cut into wedges to fit feed tube. Slice, using medium pressure with pusher. Use in salads, relishes, and soups.
1 1-pound head cabbage = 4 to 5 cups sliced

chopped

Place steel blade in work bowl. Core cabbage; cut into 1-inch pieces. Place up to 1 cup pieces in work bowl. Process with on/off turns till chopped to desired size. Use in salads, relishes, and soups.
1 1-pound head cabbage = 4 to 5 cups chopped

vegetables continued

carrots

sliced
Place slicing disk in work bowl. Cut carrots into equal lengths about 1 inch shorter than height of feed tube. Place in feed tube, as shown above. Wedge the last one in for tight fit (keeps pieces straight vertically). Slice, using firm pressure with pusher. Cook and serve or use in casseroles, soups, stews, and salads.
6 medium (1 pound) = 3 cups sliced

chopped
Place steel blade in work bowl. Cut carrots into 1-inch pieces. Place up to 1 cup pieces in work bowl. Process with on/off turns till chopped to desired size. Use in relishes, casseroles, baked goods, and salads.
6 medium (1 pound) = 3 cups chopped

shredded
Place shredding disk in work bowl. Cut carrots into lengths to fit width of feed tube. Place carrots horizontally in feed tube. Shred, using firm pressure with pusher. Use in salads, relishes, casseroles, and baked goods.
6 medium (1 pound) = 3 cups shredded

cauliflower

sliced
Place slicing disk in work bowl. Remove leaves and woody stem from cauliflower. Break head into flowerets to fit feed tube; stack flowerets horizontally in feed tube, as shown above. Slice, using light pressure with pusher. (Processing will give nice slices plus crumbles.) Use in salads, casseroles, soups, and stir-fry cooking.
1 1-pound head cauliflower = 4 cups sliced

celery

sliced
Place slicing disk in work bowl. Remove strings from celery, if desired. Cut celery into equal lengths about 1 inch shorter than height of feed tube. Place in feed tube (see illustration for *carrots, sliced*). Wedge in last piece for tight fit (keeps pieces straight vertically). Slice, using medium pressure with pusher. Use in salads, main dishes, and stir-fry cooking.
3 stalks = 1 cup sliced

chopped
Place steel blade in work bowl. Remove strings from celery, if desired. Cut celery into 1-inch pieces; place up to 1 cup pieces in work bowl. Process with on/off turns till chopped to desired size, as shown above. Use in sandwich fillings, stuffings, main dishes, and sauces.
3 stalks = 1 cup chopped

chives

chopped
Place steel blade in work bowl. Cut chives into 1-inch lengths; place up to 1 cup pieces in work bowl. Process with on/off turns till chopped to desired size. Use in soups, spreads, dips, and flavored butters.

cucumbers

sliced
Place slicing disk in work bowl. Peel cucumbers, if desired. Trim or halve lengthwise to fit feed tube, cut into equal lengths, about 1 inch shorter than height of feed tube. Place in feed tube as shown above. Slice, using medium pressure with pusher (slices will be thin). If processor doesn't slice through peel, try placing cucumber pieces in feed tube with peel facing center of work bowl. Use in salads.
1 medium = 2 cups sliced

chopped
Place steel blade in work bowl. Peel cucumbers, if desired. Cut into 1-inch pieces; remove seeds. Place up to 1 cup pieces in work bowl. Process with on/off turns till chopped to desired size; drain, if desired. Use in relishes, salads, dips, and spreads.
1 medium = 1 cup chopped

shredded
Place shredding disk in work bowl. Peel cucumbers, if desired; halve lengthwise and remove seeds. Cut into equal lengths about 1 inch shorter than height of feed tube. Place in feed tube, as shown above. Shred, using medium pressure with pusher; drain. Use in salads, dips, and spreads.
1 medium = 2 cups shredded

eggplant

sliced
Place slicing disk in work bowl. Cut off cap and bottom of eggplant; peel, if desired. Cut eggplant into halves, quarters, or pieces to fit feed tube; place in feed tube (if unpeeled, place peel side toward center of work bowl). Slice, using light pressure with pusher. Use in main dishes or deep fry and serve as an appetizer.
½ medium eggplant (8 ounces) = 2 cups sliced

chopped
Place steel blade in work bowl. Cut off cap and bottom of eggplant; peel, if desired. Cut eggplant into 1-inch pieces; place up to 1 cup pieces in work bowl. Process with on/off turns till chopped to desired size. Use in relishes and sauces.
½ medium eggplant (8 ounces) = 1½ cups chopped

vegetables continued

leeks

sliced
Place slicing disk in work bowl. Trim leeks (the white portion is more tender than the green portion). Cut into equal lengths about 1 inch shorter than height of feed tube. Place in feed tube, as shown above, wedging in last one for tight fit (keeps pieces straight vertically). Slice, using medium pressure with pusher. Use in soups, sauces, salads, and main dishes.
8 ounces = 3 cups sliced

chopped
Place steel blade in work bowl. Trim leeks (white portion is more tender than green portion); cut into 1-inch lengths. Place up to 1 cup pieces in work bowl; process with on/off turns till chopped to desired size. Use in sauces, salads, soups, and main dishes.
8 ounces = 3 cups sliced

lettuce

sliced
Place slicing disk in work bowl. Core and cut head lettuce into wedges to fit feed tube; place in feed tube. Slice, using light pressure with pusher. Use in seafood cocktails, layered salads, tacos, and sandwich fillings.

chopped
Place steel blade in work bowl. Tear up lettuce or cut into chunks (core head lettuce). Place up to 2 cups lettuce in work bowl; process with on/off turns till chopped to desired size. Use in layered salads and tacos.
2 cups cut up or torn lettuce = 1 cup chopped

mushrooms

sliced
Place slicing disk in work bowl. Arrange mushrooms horizontally in feed tube, stacking atop each other to within about 1 inch of top of feed tube, as shown above. Slice, using medium pressure with pusher. Use in sauces, main dishes, and salads.
8 ounces = 2½ to 3 cups sliced

chopped
Place steel blade in work bowl. Halve large mushrooms. Place up to 1 cup mushrooms in work bowl. Process with on/off turns till chopped to desired size. Use in fillings, stuffings, and main dishes.
8 ounces = 2 cups chopped

okra

sliced
Place slicing disk in work bowl. Remove stems from okra. Cut okra into equal lengths about 1 inch shorter than height of feed tube, if necessary. Place vertically in feed tube, wedging in last one for tight fit (keeps pieces straight vertically). Slice, using medium pressure with pusher (slices will be thinner than those usually purchased, so cooking time will be less). Use in soups, stews, creole dishes, and casseroles.
8 ounces okra = 2½ cups sliced

onions

sliced
Place slicing disk in work bowl. Peel onions; halve large onions vertically. Place in feed tube, as shown above; or wedge in 2 halves of small onion as shown on page 11. Slice, using medium pressure with pusher. Use in soups, sauces, salads, and casseroles.
1 medium onion (5 ounces) = 1 to 1⅓ cups sliced

chopped
Place steel blade in work bowl. Peel onions; cut into 1-inch pieces (small to medium onions may be quartered). Place up to 1 cup pieces in work bowl. Process with on/off turns till chopped to desired size. If desired, store, covered, in refrigerator or freeze in 1-cup amounts in freezer containers. Use in casseroles, soups, sauces, and stuffings.
1 medium onion (5 ounces) = ½ cup chopped

onions (green)

sliced
Place slicing disk in work bowl. Trim onions; cut into equal lengths about 1 inch shorter than height of feed tube. Place in feed tube, as shown in illustration for *leeks, sliced;* wedge last one in for tight fit (keeps pieces straight vertically). Slice, using medium pressure with pusher. Use in salads, dips, spreads, and main dishes.

chopped
Place steel blade in work bowl. Trim onions; cut into 1-inch lengths. Place up to 1 cup pieces in work bowl. Process with on/off turns till chopped to desired size. Use in dips, spreads, soups, and casseroles.

vegetables continued

parsley

chopped
Place steel blade in work bowl. Rinse parsley; thoroughly pat dry with paper toweling. Remove stems. Place up to 1 cup lightly packed parsley in work bowl; process with on/off turns till chopped to desired size. Use in dips, spreads, sandwich fillings, and main dishes.

parsnips

sliced
Place slicing disk in work bowl. Cut parsnips into equal lengths about 1 inch shorter than height of feed tube. Place vertically in feed tube, wedging in last one for tight fit (keeps pieces straight vertically). Slice, using firm pressure with pusher. Use in soups and main dishes.

peppers

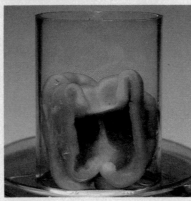

sliced
Place slicing disk in work bowl. Halve or quarter peppers lengthwise; remove stems, seeds, and inner membranes. Place 2 halves in feed tube with peel side towards center of work bowl, as shown above. Slice, using medium pressure with pusher. Use in salads, sauces, pizza, and main dishes.
1 medium pepper = ¾ cup sliced

chopped
Place steel blade in work bowl. Remove stems, seeds, and inner membranes; cut peppers into 1-inch pieces. Place up to 1 cup pieces in work bowl. Process with on/off turns till chopped to desired size. Use in relishes, sauces, and main dishes.
1 medium pepper = ¾ cup chopped

pimientos

chopped
Place steel blade in work bowl. Drain canned whole pimientos; place up to 1 cup in work bowl. Process with on/off turns till chopped to desired size. Use in dips, spreads, salads, sauces, and casseroles.

potatoes (uncooked)

sliced
Place slicing disk in work bowl. Peel potatoes, if desired; halve to fit feed tube, if necessary. Place in feed tube. Slice, using medium pressure with pusher. Fry or use in soups and casseroles.
1 small potato (4 ounces) = ¾ cup sliced

chopped
Place steel blade in work bowl. Peel potatoes; cut into 1-inch pieces. Place up to 1 cup pieces in work bowl. Process with on/off turns till chopped to desired size. Fry or use in casseroles and soups.
1 small potato (4 ounces) = ⅔ cup chopped

shredded
Place shredding disk in work bowl. Peel potatoes; halve to fit feed tube, if necessary. Place in feed tube. Shred, using medium pressure with pusher. Pan-fry or use in potato pancakes, soups, and main dishes.
1 small potato (4 ounces) = ¾ cup shredded

potatoes (cooked)

sliced

Some machines give satisfactory cooked potato slices; other machines give only crumbles.

Use whole, firm (not baking) potatoes. In covered pan cook in boiling salted water for 25 to 30 minutes or just till tender. Drain; chill. Place slicing disk in work bowl. Peel potatoes; halve to fit feed tube, if necessary. Place potatoes in feed tube. Slice, using medium pressure with pusher. Use for potato salad and main dishes.

mashed

Peel and quarter baking potatoes. In covered pan cook in enough boiling salted water to cover for about 25 minutes or till tender. Drain, reserving cooking liquid; cool slightly. Place steel blade in work bowl. Add up to 2 cups of the cooked potato plus 3 to 4 tablespoons cooking liquid or milk. Process till smooth, stopping to scrape sides of bowl as necessary. Season to taste.
3 medium potatoes (1 pound) = 2 cups mashed

potatoes (sweet)

mashed

Remove ends and woody portions from sweet potatoes. In covered pan cook in enough boiling salted water to cover for 30 to 40 minutes or till tender. Drain and cool slightly; peel. Place steel blade in work bowl; add up to 2 cups cooked potato. Process till smooth, scraping sides of work bowl as needed. Season to taste.
3 medium (1 pound) = 2 cups mashed

pumpkin

mashed

Halve pumpkin; remove seeds and strings. Place, cut side down, in baking pan; cover with foil. Bake in 350° oven for 30 minutes. Turn cut side up; bake, covered, about 45 minutes more or till tender. Scoop out pulp; discard peel. Place steel blade in work bowl. Add up to 2 cups cooked pumpkin. Process till smooth, scraping down sides of work bowl as needed. Use for pies, cakes, breads, and cookies.
1 2-pound pumpkin = 2 cups cooked and mashed

radishes

sliced

Place slicing disk in work bowl. Trim radishes; stack radishes in feed tube, cut side down. Slice, using medium pressure with pusher. Use in salads and relishes.

rutabagas

sliced

Place slicing disk in work bowl. Peel rutabagas; trim to fit feed tube. Place in feed tube; slice, using medium pressure with pusher. Use in soups and stews.

chopped

Place steel blade in work bowl. Peel rutabagas; cut into 1-inch pieces. Place up to 1 cup pieces in work bowl. Process with on/off turns till chopped to desired size. Use in soups, stews, and casseroles.

spinach

chopped

Place steel blade in work bowl. Remove spinach stems; wash leaves and dry thoroughly. Tear up large leaves. Place up to 2 cups lightly packed spinach in work bowl. Process with on/off turns till chopped to desired size. Use in fillings, appetizers, soups, and main dishes.

vegetables continued

squash (zucchini and other summer)

sliced
Place slicing disk in work bowl. Cut ends from squash; cut squash into equal lengths about 1 inch shorter than height of feed tube. Halve lengthwise, if necessary, to fit feed tube; place vertically in feed tube with peel toward center of work bowl. Slice, using medium pressure with pusher. Cook and serve or use in casseroles and salads.
1 pound = 4 cups sliced

chopped
Place steel blade in work bowl. Cut ends from squash; cut squash into 1-inch pieces. Place up to 1 cup pieces in work bowl. Process with on/off turns till chopped to desired size. Use in relishes, sauces, main dishes, and baked goods.
1 pound = 3 cups chopped

shredded
Place shredding disk in work bowl. Cut ends from squash; cut squash into lengths about 1 inch shorter than height of feed tube. Halve lengthwise, if necessary, to fit in feed tube. Place vertically in feed tube. Shred, using medium pressure with pusher. Use in cakes, quick breads, and relishes.
1 pound = 3 cups shredded

squash (winter)

mashed
Halve squash; remove seeds and strings. Place halves, cut side down, in baking pan. Cover with foil; bake in 350° oven for 30 minutes. Turn cut side up; bake, covered, till tender (20 to 30 minutes more for acorn, buttercup, or butternut squash; 45 to 50 minutes more for hubbard squash). Scoop out pulp; discard peel. Place steel blade in work bowl. Add up to 2 cups of the cooked squash. Process till smooth, scraping down sides of work bowl as needed. Season to taste with butter or margarine, salt, and pepper.
1 pound = 1 cup mashed

tomatoes

chopped
Place steel blade in work bowl. Select firm green or ripe tomatoes; core. Remove peel and seeds, if desired. Halve or quarter tomatoes. Place up to 1 cup pieces in work bowl. Process with on/off turns till chopped to desired size. Use in relishes, sauces, and jams.
1 medium = ¾ cup chopped

turnips

sliced
Place slicing disk in work bowl. Peel turnips; halve, if necessary, to fit feed tube. Place in feed tube. Slice, using medium pressure with pusher. Use in soups, stews, and side dishes.

chopped
Place steel blade in work bowl. Peel turnips; cut into 1-inch pieces. Place up to 1 cup pieces in work bowl. Process with on/off turns till chopped to desired size. Use in soups, stews, and casseroles.

water chestnuts

sliced
Place slicing disk in work bowl. Drain canned whole water chestnuts; drop into feed tube, as shown in top photo, above. Slice, using light pressure with pusher. Use in salads and stir-fry cooking.
1 8-ounce can whole water chestnuts = 1 cup sliced

chopped
Place steel blade in work bowl. Drain canned whole water chestnuts. Place up to 1 cup in work bowl. Process with on/off turns till chopped to desired size. Use in appetizers, spreads, dips, egg rolls, and wontons.
1 8-ounce can water chestnuts = 1 cup chopped

miscellaneous

bread

soft crumbs
Place steel blade in work bowl. Tear bread into pieces; place up to 3 slices torn bread in work bowl. Process till finely crumbled. Use in meat loaf and crumb toppings.
1 slice soft bread = ¾ cup crumbs

dry crumbs
Place steel blade in work bowl. Break dry bread into 2-inch pieces; add up to 3 slices broken bread to work bowl. Process till finely crumbled. Use in meat loaves, meatballs, and as a crumb coating for fried or baked foods.
1 slice dry bread = ¼ cup crumbs

butter mints

crushed
Place steel blade in work bowl. Start machine; gradually add mints through feed tube, holding hand over tube to prevent candy from flying out. Process till very finely crushed. Use in frozen salads and desserts.

chips

crushed
Place steel blade in work bowl. Add potato, corn, or tortilla chips, filling work bowl no more than ⅓ full. Process with on/off turns to desired fineness. Use atop casseroles.

chocolate

chopped
Some machines will give quite a bit of chocolate powder as well as chopped chocolate.
Place steel blade in work bowl. Cut well-chilled chocolate into 1-inch pieces (or use chilled semisweet or milk chocolate pieces). Start machine; gradually add chocolate pieces through feed tube, holding hand over tube to prevent chocolate from flying out (or place up to 1 cup chocolate pieces in work bowl). Process to desired fineness. Use in desserts.

cinnamon candy

crushed
Place steel blade in work bowl. Start machine; pour candies through feed tube, holding hand over tube to prevent candy from flying out. Process till finely crushed. Use in frozen salads and desserts.

coconut

finely chopped
Place steel blade in work bowl. Puncture eyes of coconut; drain. Pound off outer shell; remove brown skin. Cut coconut into 1-inch pieces; place up to 1 cup pieces in work bowl. Process till finely chopped. Use in salads, desserts, and baked goods.
1 1¼-pound coconut = 2½ cups

shredded
Place shredding disk in work bowl. Puncture eyes of coconut; drain. Pound off outer shell; remove brown skin. Cut coconut into pieces to fit feed tube. Shred, using firm pressure with pusher. Use in salads, desserts, and baked goods; see tip on page 92.
1 1¼-pound coconut = 2½ cups

miscellaneous continued

cookies

crushed
Place steel blade in work bowl. Add cookies (break up large ones), filling up to ⅓ full. Process till finely crushed. Use for crumb crusts. 19 chocolate wafers (½ of 8½-ounce package) = 1 cup fine crumbs. 15 gingersnaps = 1 cup fine crumbs 24 vanilla wafers = 1 cup fine crumbs

corn flakes

crushed
Place steel blade in work bowl; add up to 1 cup corn flakes. Process till finely crushed. Use in meat loaves or as crumb coating.

crackers

crushed
Place steel blade in work bowl; add crackers, breaking larger ones in half. Fill work bowl no more than ⅓ full. Process till finely crushed. Use in meat loaves, crumb crusts, desserts, and crumb toppings.
28 square saltines (2 inch) = 1 cup fine crumbs
24 rich round crackers = 1 cup fine crumbs
14 graham cracker squares = 1 cup fine crumbs

garlic

minced
Place steel blade in work bowl. Peel garlic cloves; halve or quarter. Start machine; add garlic through feed tube, holding hand over tube to prevent garlic from flying out. Process till very finely chopped, scraping sides of bowl as needed. Garlic seldom is processed alone like this. Usually it is added to the work bowl with another ingredient, such as a cut-up onion, and processed. Use in dips, sauces, soups, and main dishes.

gingerroot

minced
Place steel blade in work bowl. Peel gingerroot; cut into 1-inch pieces. Place up to 1 cup pieces in work bowl; process till very finely chopped, scraping down sides of bowl as needed. Use in stir-fry cooking and other Oriental dishes.

hard candies

crushed
Place steel blade in work bowl. If using peppermint stick candy, break into 1-inch pieces. Start machine; gradually add candy pieces through feed tube, holding hand over tube to prevent candy from flying out. Process till very finely crushed. Use in frozen salads, refrigerator pies, puddings, or ice cream.

horseradish root

minced
Place steel blade in work bowl. Peel horseradish root; cut into 1-inch pieces. Place up to 1 cup pieces in work bowl; process till very finely chopped. When uncovering the bowl, lift cover away from you as the aroma of pure minced horseradish is quite strong. Use in sauces and dips; also see tip on page 76.

ice

crushed
Follow manufacturer's directions for crushing ice. It is not recommended for many processors. Use in beverages.

nuts

coarsely chopped
Place steel blade in work bowl. Add up to 1 cup nutmeats. Process with on/off turns till chopped to desired size, as shown above. If desired, store, covered, in refrigerator or freezer. Use in salads, desserts, and baked goods. 4 ounces nuts = 1 cup chopped

finely ground
Place steel blade in work bowl; add up to 1 cup nutmeats. Process till very finely chopped; be careful not to overprocess or nuts start to form a butter. If desired, store, covered, in refrigerator or freezer. Use in tortes, cakes, and other baked goods.
To form butter
See tip on page 51.

olives

sliced
Place slicing disk in work bowl. Drop pitted whole olives into feed tube. Slice, using medium pressure with pusher. For more uniform slices, arrange olives, flattest side down in single layer in feed tube. Slice, using medium pressure with pusher. Use in salads, salad dressings, sauces, and main dishes.

chopped
Place steel blade in work bowl; add up to 1 cup pitted whole olives. Process with on/off turns till chopped to desired size. Use in main dishes, sandwich fillings, and relishes.

pickles

sliced
Place slicing disk in work bowl. Cut ends from whole pickles; place in feed tube. Slice using medium pressure with pusher. Serve with sandwiches or on relish tray.

chopped
Place steel blade in work bowl. Cut ends from whole pickles; cut pickles into 1-inch pieces. Place up to 1 cup pieces in work bowl. Process with on/off turns till chopped to desired size. Use in sandwich fillings, spreads, dips, and salad dressings.

toffee bars

crushed
Place steel blade in work bowl. Cut chilled chocolate-covered English toffee bars into 1-inch pieces. Start machine; gradually add candy through feed tube, holding hand over tube to prevent candy from flying out. Process till finely crushed. Use in cookies and desserts.

adapting favorite recipes

You can use your food processor for the total preparation of many foods. The recipes on pages 38 to 43 offer guidelines for adapting your own favorites.

Cranberry-Banana Bread (see recipe, page 40)

Whole Wheat Bread (see recipe, page 39)

Everyday Meat
Loaf (see recipe
page 38)

Nut Butter
Cookies (see
recipe, page 41)

ground meat mixtures

Making ground meat mixtures in the processor means you can control the amount of fat in the meat and the extent to which the meat is chopped. However, the flavor and texture of the meat will be somewhat different from the purchased ground meat that you are used to using.

Lean meat with almost no fat can be used for a special diet. For ordinary use, remember that fat adds flavor and juiciness; so some fat should be included along with the lean meat. Also, ground meat without fat is usually tougher.

For the most evenly chopped mixture, cut the meat into uniform size pieces, trimming away all gristle and bone. Don't process more than ½ pound (1 cup) at a time. If you do, some meat will be chopped much finer than the rest. It takes practice to judge how far to carry the processing. For comparison, see photo for *beef (uncooked) chopped*, page 22.

When combining the meat with other ingredients, use on/off turns; avoid overprocessing.

Everyday Meat Loaf

1½ pounds boneless beef chuck, gristle and excess fat removed
¼ small onion, cut up
3 slices dry bread, broken
2 eggs
¾ cup milk
1 teaspoon salt
½ teaspoon ground sage
⅓ cup catsup
¼ cup packed brown sugar
2 teaspoons prepared mustard

Cut meat into 1-inch pieces. Insert steel blade in work bowl; add ⅓ of the meat. Process till chopped (see photo, page 22); remove. Repeat with another ⅓ of meat. Add rest of meat, onion, bread, eggs, milk, salt, sage, and dash *pepper*. Process till meat is chopped and ingredients are mixed. Return rest of chopped meat; process just till all ingredients are well mixed (see photo, below). Pat mixture into 8x4x2-inch loaf dish. Bake in 350° oven for 1 hour.

Meanwhile, combine catsup, brown sugar, and mustard; pour over meat loaf. Bake 15 to 20 minutes more. Makes 6 servings.

yeast breads

When making yeast breads remember that most processors can't handle more than 3 cups of flour. You may need to cut your recipe in half and prepare consecutive batches to bake the desired number of loaves. Both conventional and easy-mix recipes can be used.

Do not process the dough more than 60 seconds; if it hasn't formed a ball, shape by hand. If the motor begins to slow down, quickly add a little more flour. This should free the dough from the blade so the motor can return to normal speed.

Whole Wheat Bread

- 1 **package active dry yeast**
- 1 **cup warm water (115°)**
- 2 **tablespoons brown sugar**
- 1½ **cups all-purpose flour**
- 1½ **cups whole wheat flour**
- 2 **tablespoons shortening**
- 1 **teaspoon salt**

Conventional Method: Dissolve yeast in water; add sugar. Combine flours. Insert steel blade; add *2 cups* flour mixture, the shortening, and the salt. Process with on/off turns till resembles cornmeal. Add ½ *cup* yeast mixture; process with 4 on/off turns. Add remaining yeast mixture; repeat 4 on/off turns.

Add remaining flour mixture; process with 4 on/off turns. Let machine run 15 seconds or till ball of dough forms (see photo, below). If dough seems sticky, add 1 to 2 tablespoons all-purpose flour. *Do not process more than 60 seconds.*

Place dough in greased bowl; turn once to grease surface. Cover; let rise in warm place till double (45 to 60 minutes). Punch down. Shape into loaf; place in greased 8x4x2-inch loaf pan. Cover; let rise till double (30 to 45 minutes).

Bake in 375° oven about 45 minutes. If top browns too quickly, cover with foil the last 20 minutes. Cool on wire rack. Makes 1.

Easy-Mix Method: Use ingredients as above. Place steel blade in work bowl; add *2 cups* flour mixture, dry yeast, sugar, shortening, and salt. Process with 4 on/off turns till resembles cornmeal. Add ½ *cup* water; process with 4 on/off turns. Add remaining ½ cup water; process with 4 on/off turns. Add rest of flour mixture; continue as above.

quick breads

The secret to success in making quick breads with a food processor is to avoid overprocessing because it makes the bread tough.

When choosing the recipe, remember that most processors can't handle a batter using more than 3 cups of flour. Halve recipes and mix up consecutive batches if a larger yield is desired.

Often nuts and fruits in breads need to be processed before being added. Do them first, starting with the driest, such as nuts.

Next, process the sugar, butter, egg, and liquid till smooth.

Thoroughly stir together the flour, leavening, and spices in a mixing bowl. (This will help ensure that the leavening is evenly distributed throughout the batter.) Add to the sugar-butter mixture and process only till the flour is no longer visible. This should take only 2 or 3 on/off turns. If a little flour is still visible, stir it in by hand.

Cranberry-Banana Bread

     1   cup pecans
    1½   cups fresh *or* frozen cranberries
     1   large fully ripe banana, cut up
     1   cup sugar
     ¼   cup butter, cut into pieces
     ¼   cup milk
     1   egg
     2   1-inch strips orange peel (cut with vegetable peeler)
     2   cups all-purpose flour
     1   tablespoon baking powder
     ¾   teaspoon ground cinnamon
     ½   teaspoon salt

Place steel blade in work bowl; add pecans. Process with on/off turns till finely chopped; remove. Reinsert steel blade; add cranberries. Process with on/off turns till finely chopped; remove and drain, if necessary.

Rinse work bowl; reinsert steel blade. Add banana, sugar, butter, milk, egg, and orange peel; process till smooth. Stir together the flour, baking powder, cinnamon, and salt; add to work bowl. Process with 3 on/off turns or just till flour disappears (see photo, below). *Do not overmix.* Transfer to mixing bowl; gently stir in pecans and cranberries. (Adding cranberries and processing to mix tints batter pink.) Turn into greased 9x5x3-inch loaf pan. Bake in 350° oven for 60 to 65 minutes. Cool 10 minutes in pan; remove and cool thoroughly. Makes 1.

cookies

Making cookies with a processor is similar to making them with an electric mixer. You will need to reduce recipes, if necessary, to avoid adding more than 3 cups of flour.

Check for nuts, fruits, or other ingredients that need to be processed before they can be added to the batter. Do them first.

After that, follow the recipe as you would conventionally, starting with the butter-sugar-egg mixture. Butter or margarine is better processed cold from the refrigerator rather than softened to room temperature.

In a mixing bowl stir together the flour, leavening, and spices. (This will help ensure that the leavening is evenly distributed throughout the batter.) Add to the butter-sugar-egg mixture.

Use your judgment when adding rolled oats, other cereals, chocolate pieces, or chopped fruits. If the conventional recipe directs you to *stir* them in at the end, it's a good idea to do the same when using the processor.

Nut Butter Cookies

½ cup granulated sugar
½ cup packed brown sugar
½ cup **Nut Butter** (see recipe, page 51)*
½ cup **butter** *or* **margarine**
1 egg
½ teaspoon vanilla
1¼ cups all-purpose flour
¾ teaspoon baking soda
¼ teaspoon salt

Place steel blade in work bowl; add sugars, Nut Butter, butter or margarine, egg, and vanilla. Process till creamy. Stir together the flour, baking soda, and salt; add to creamed mixture. Process just till flour is mixed in (see photo, below).

Shape dough into 1-inch balls; place 2 inches apart on ungreased cookie sheet. Crisscross with fork tines to flatten slightly. Bake in 375° oven for 10 to 12 minutes. Cool slightly; remove from pan and cool on wire rack. Makes 3 dozen.

*To make ½ cup Nut Butter, place steel blade in work bowl; add 1 cup *nuts*. Process 4 to 5 minutes or till butter forms, scraping down sides of bowl occasionally to make sure all of mixture is evenly blended. Add sugars, butter, egg, and vanilla; continue as above.

pastry

When making pastry, you can use either the steel blade or the plastic blade. Check the recipe before starting. Most processors can't handle a dough made with more than 3 cups of flour.

The most noticeable difference in using the processor for pastry is that less water is needed — about half as much, usually.

Be sure to use ice cold water; that is, water chilled with ice cubes. Process the flour, butter, and salt. Then measure the necessary amount of ice cold water in a liquid measuring cup and add by pouring it through the feed tube into the mixture.

Process with only 1 or 2 on/off turns. Do not process further, even if not all of the mixture is moistened. Further processing will make the pastry tough.

Turn the dough out onto a floured surface and shape by hand into a ball before rolling out. You may need to sprinkle a little water over the dough if it is too dry to hold together in a ball.

For pastry made with shortening or lard, see recipe on page 92.

Butter Pastry

   2   cups all-purpose flour
   ¾   cup cold butter, cut into chunks
   ½   teaspoon salt
   3   tablespoons ice cold water

Place steel blade in work bowl; add the flour, chunks of cold butter, and salt. Process with on/off turns till most of mixture resembles cornmeal but a few larger-size pieces remain.

Have the 3 tablespoons ice cold water in a cup. With machine running, quickly pour water through feed tube. Stop machine; scrape sides of work bowl. Process with 2 on/off turns. Mixture may not all be moistened (see photo, below).

Turn pastry out onto lightly floured surface; shape into 2 equal balls. (If dough is too dry to hold together in ball, sprinkle up to 1 tablespoon ice cold water atop and mix in by hand.) Roll out for either single or double crust pastry, following the directions on page 92. Makes two 9-inch single-crust pastries or one 9-inch double-crust pastry.

hollandaise sauce

It is hard to make general rules for adapting sauce recipes to processor preparation. So, be prepared to do some experimenting. The differences of Hollandaise Sauce are explained here; see pages 74 to 79 for other processor sauce recipes to compare with your own.

The main difference in making Hollandaise Sauce in the processor is the order in which the ingredients are assembled. Instead of the butter and egg yolks being cooked together, then the lemon juice being added, the eggs and lemon juice are processed till smooth and then the melted butter is added

For best results, the eggs should be at room temperature before starting. If you don't have time to let them set out, place them in a bowl of warm water for about 5 minutes. When heating the butter or margarine, watch carefully and add it just when it's ready to boil.

If the sauce can't be served immediately, keep it warm in a double boiler set over hot water (it will curdle if placed over water that is too hot.)

Hollandaise Sauce

  4 **egg yolks (room temperature)**
  2 **tablespoons lemon juice**
     Dash cayenne
  ½ **cup butter *or* margarine**

Place steel blade in work bowl; add egg yolks, lemon juice, and cayenne. Process with on/off turns just till ingredients are blended. Heat butter or margarine almost to boiling. With machine running, gradually pour hot butter through feed tube in a steady stream. Process about 3 minutes or till thick and fluffy (see photo, below). Scrape down sides of bowl as needed. Serve immediately or keep warm in a double boiler set over hot (not boiling) water. Makes about ¾ cup.

Cream Cheese Hollandaise: Prepare Hollandaise Sauce as above *except* use only 3 egg yolks and only 1 tablespoon lemon juice. Add one 3-ounce package *cream cheese*, cubed, to the yolk mixture. Process with on/off turns till blended; add the hot butter and continue as above. Makes 1 cup.

appetizers, snacks, & spreads

Chicken Liver Pâté

1 pound chicken livers
¼ cup chopped onion
2 tablespoons butter *or* margarine
3 tablespoons mayonnaise *or* salad dressing
2 tablespoons butter *or* margarine
2 tablespoons lemon juice
8 to 10 drops bottled hot pepper sauce
½ teaspoon salt
½ teaspoon dry mustard
Dash pepper
Chopped hard-cooked egg *or* yolk, snipped chives, *or* parsley sprigs (optional)
Assorted crackers

In heavy skillet cook livers and onion in 2 tablespoons butter or margarine, covered, over medium-high heat about 5 minutes or till livers are no longer pink; stir occasionally. Drain, reserving 3 tablespoons liquid.

Place steel blade in work bowl. Add livers and reserved liquid. Process till finely chopped. Add mayonnaise or salad dressing, 2 tablespoons butter or margarine, lemon juice, hot pepper sauce, salt, mustard, and pepper. Process till smooth.

Turn into well-oiled 2-cup mold or bowl. Cover; chill 6 hours or overnight. Carefully unmold. If desired, garnish with chopped hard-cooked egg or yolk and snipped chives or parsley sprigs. Serve with assorted crackers. Makes about 1⅔ cups.

Clockwise from top left: Chicken Liver Pâté, Ham and Kraut Snacks, Salmon Dip (see recipe, page 48), Sunflower-Nut Spread (see recipe, page 51), and Dessert Cheese Ball.

Ham and Kraut Snacks

2 slices dry bread, broken
½ medium onion, cut into 1-inch pieces
1 small clove garlic, cut up
1 tablespoon butter *or* margarine
5 ounces fully cooked ham, cut into 1-inch pieces (1 cup)
¼ cup lightly packed parsley (stems removed)
1 14-ounce can sauerkraut
½ cup packaged pancake mix
Cooking oil *or* shortening for deep-fat frying
Horseradish-Mustard Sauce (see recipe, page 76) (optional)

Place steel blade in work bowl; add dry bread pieces. Process till very finely crushed; empty bowl and set bread crumbs aside. Reinsert steel blade in work bowl; add onion and garlic. Process with on/off turns till finely chopped. Cook onion and garlic in butter or margarine till tender but not brown.

Meanwhile, reinsert steel blade in work bowl; add ham and parsley. Process with on/off turns till finely chopped. Remove to a mixing bowl. Drain sauerkraut, reserving ⅓ cup liquid. Reinsert steel blade in work bowl; add sauerkraut. Process with on/off turns till chopped. Add to ham in mixing bowl; add onion-garlic mixture and the reserved sauerkraut liquid. Mix well. Add the pancake mix; stir till combined. Cover and chill.

With a tablespoon measure, form mixture into balls; roll in reserved bread crumbs. Fry 4 to 6 at a time in deep hot oil or shortening (365°) for 1½ to 2 minutes or till crisp and golden brown. Serve hot with Horseradish-Mustard Sauce for dipping, if desired. Makes about 3 dozen.

Dessert Cheese Ball

Shaping in cheesecloth gives this cheese ball a textured surface —

2 cups cream-style cottage cheese (16 ounces)
1 3-ounce package cream cheese, quartered
2 ounces blue cheese, cut into 1-inch pieces
1 cup whipping cream
Assorted crackers
Sliced apples *and* pears
Lemon juice *or* ascorbic acid color keeper

Place steel blade in work bowl; add cottage cheese, cream cheese, and blue cheese. Process till mixture is smooth and creamy, stopping as needed to scrape down sides of work bowl.

With machine running, gradually pour whipping cream through feed tube. Process about 25 seconds or just till mixture is thickened.

Line a sieve or colander with several thicknesses of cheesecloth; set in a bowl. Pour in cheese mixture. Tie cheesecloth at top. Let drain overnight in refrigerator.

Untie cloth; turn cheese ball out onto serving platter. Remove cheesecloth. Decorate top of cheese with lemon or mint leaves, if desired. Surround cheese with assorted crackers and with apples and pears brushed lightly with lemon juice or ascorbic acid color keeper. Makes 6 to 8 servings.

Chilled Chicken Loaf

- 5 slices bacon
- 1½ cups fresh mushrooms
- 4 green onions, cut into 1-inch pieces
- 8 ounces chicken livers
- 3 tablespoons butter
- ½ teaspoon salt
- ¼ teaspoon dried thyme, crushed
- ⅛ teaspoon pepper
- 8 ounces boneless veal
- 8 ounces skinned and boned uncooked chicken breasts
- 8 ounces bulk pork sausage
- ⅓ cup dry white wine
- 1 egg

Cook bacon till brown but not crisp; drain. Arrange slices crosswise across bottom and up sides of 8x4x2-inch loaf pan.

Place steel blade in work bowl; add mushrooms and green onions. Process with on/off turns till finely chopped. In skillet cook chopped vegetables and livers in butter over medium-high heat about 5 minutes or till livers are no longer pink; stir occasionally. Stir in salt, thyme, and pepper; cool.

Cut veal and chicken into 1-inch pieces. Reinsert steel blade; add veal. Process with on/off turns till finely chopped; transfer to mixing bowl. Reinsert steel blade; add chicken. Process till finely chopped. Add to veal; add sausage and wine. Mix well.

Reinsert steel blade; add cooled liver mixture. Process till nearly smooth. With machine running, add egg through feed tube. Process till smooth. Spread *half* of the liver mixture into bacon-lined pan. Top with veal mixture, then remaining liver mixture, spreading evenly. Bake in 350° oven for 1½ hours. Remove from oven. Chill as directed in tip, right. Remove from pan; cut into slices. Makes 8 servings (16 appetizer servings).

terrines

The term "terrine" refers to a meat, fish, or game mixture similar to pâté, which is baked and then chilled. The baking dish itself also may be called a terrine.

Terrines often have a bacon overlay that results from lining the pan with partially cooked bacon slices. After baking and chilling, the bacon may have some fat visible on its surface. Uncooked bacon can be used; but even after baking, the bacon may have a slightly uncooked appearance.

Chilling under weights helps give the loaf the desired firm texture. After baking, carefully drain off the excess fat and juices, leaving the meat in the pan. Cover surface of hot meat with foil or waxed paper. Place another loaf pan containing a weight (such as a can of vegetables) atop hot meat. Let cool, then chill at least 8 hours.

To remove loaf, loosen edges with spatula; dip pan into hot water a few seconds, then invert and remove.

Garlic Butter

- 2 or 3 cloves garlic, halved
- ½ cup butter, cut up

Place steel blade in work bowl. With machine running, drop garlic through feed tube; process till finely chopped. Add butter; process till smooth and fluffy. Spread on French bread before heating or melt atop steaks. Makes ½ cup.

Lamb-Sausage Terrine

- 8 slices bacon
- ½ pound fully cooked ham, cut into 1-inch pieces
- 2 cups cubed cooked lamb
- ½ small onion, quartered
- 1 egg
- ¼ cup milk
- 2 tablespoons brandy
- 1 slice bread, torn
- ½ teaspoon salt
- ¼ teaspoon pepper
- ¼ teaspoon dried thyme
- ¼ teaspoon dried marjoram
- 1 pound bulk pork sausage

Cook bacon till brown but not crisp; drain. Arrange slices crosswise across bottom and up sides of 9x5x3-inch loaf pan.

Place steel blade in work bowl; add ham. Process with on/off turns till chopped; remove and set aside. Reinsert steel blade; add *1 cup* lamb. Process with on/off turns till finely chopped. Remove to mixing bowl; reinsert steel blade. Add remaining lamb and onion; process with on/off turns till finely chopped. Add to mixing bowl.

Reinsert steel blade in work bowl; add egg, milk, brandy, bread, salt, pepper, thyme, and marjoram. Process till mixture is blended. Add to lamb mixture in mixing bowl; add sausage and mix well by hand.

Pat about ⅓ of the lamb mixture (about 1½ cups) over bacon in pan. Cover with *half* of the chopped ham. Repeat layers, ending with the lamb mixture. Bake in 350° oven for 1¼ hours. Remove from oven. Chill as directed in tip, left. Makes 8 servings (16 appetizer servings).

Caper Butter

1 tablespoon drained capers
½ cup butter *or* margarine, cut into pieces

Place steel blade in work bowl; add capers. Process with on/off turns till finely chopped, scraping sides of bowl. Add butter or margarine; process till smooth and fluffy, scraping bowl as needed. Serve with fish. Refrigerate any remaining. Makes ½ cup.

Clam Shells

12 rich round crackers
1 ounce parmesan cheese, cubed (¼ cup grated)
1 medium onion, quartered
1 small green pepper, cut up
¼ cup butter *or* margarine
2 tablespoons all-purpose flour
¼ teaspoon salt
Dash worcestershire sauce
Dash bottled hot pepper sauce
1 7½-ounce can minced clams
1 tablespoon butter *or* margarine, melted

Place steel blade in work bowl; add crackers and cheese. Process till finely chopped; remove and set aside. Reinsert steel blade; add onion and green pepper. Process till chopped.

Heat ¼ cup butter in 8-inch skillet; add chopped vegetables. Cook till tender but not brown. Stir in the flour, salt, worcestershire sauce, and bottled hot pepper sauce. Add ¼ *cup* of the cracker-cheese mixture; mix well. Stir in the *undrained* clams; cook and stir till thickened and bubbly.

Divide among 6 baking shells or individual baking dishes. Combine the remaining cracker mixture and 1 tablespoon melted butter; sprinkle atop clam mixture in each shell. Bake in 350° oven about 15 minutes or till heated through. Serves 6.

Shrimp-Cheese Balls

½ cup toasted pecans *or* mixed salted nuts
2 3-ounce packages cream cheese, quartered
1 thin slice of small onion
1½ teaspoons prepared mustard
1 teaspoon lemon juice
Dash salt
Dash cayenne
1 4½-ounce can shrimp, drained

Place steel blade in work bowl; add nuts. Process till finely chopped; remove and set aside. Reinsert steel blade; add cream cheese, onion, mustard, lemon juice, salt, and cayenne. Process till smooth. Add drained shrimp; process with 2 or 3 on/off turns just till mixed. Transfer cheese mixture to covered container; chill about 2 hours. Shape chilled mixture into ½-inch balls; roll in chopped nuts. Makes 40.

Tuna-Cheese Ball

½ cup lightly packed parsley (stems removed)
½ stalk celery, cut up
1 7-ounce can tuna (water pack), drained
1 3-ounce package neufchatel cheese, quartered
2 teaspoons worcestershire sauce
1 teaspoon lemon juice
¼ teaspoon salt

Place steel blade in work bowl; add parsley. Process till finely chopped; remove and set aside. Reinsert steel blade; add celery. Process till coarsely chopped. Add the tuna, cheese, worcestershire, lemon juice, and salt. Process till well mixed; chill. Shape chilled mixture into a ball; roll in chopped parsley. Chill several hours before serving. Makes 1 cheese ball.

Guacamole

A very smooth dip —

2 ripe medium avocados, quartered, seeded, and peeled
1 tablespoon lemon juice
1 thin slice of small onion
1 clove garlic, quartered
½ teaspoon salt
Bottled hot pepper sauce (optional)
Vegetable dippers

Place steel blade in work bowl. Add avocados, lemon juice, onion, garlic, and salt. Process till smooth, scraping sides of bowl as necessary. If desired, add pepper sauce to taste. Serve immediately or transfer to bowl, covering surface of dip with clear plastic wrap to prevent discoloration; chill. Serve with fresh vegetable dippers. Makes 1¼ cups.

Hot Broccoli Dip

1 10-ounce package frozen chopped broccoli
1 cup dairy sour cream
1 teaspoon instant beef bouillon granules
1 teaspoon worcestershire sauce
¼ teaspoon garlic salt
Parsley sprigs (optional)
Bread sticks or crackers

In 2-quart saucepan cook broccoli according to package directions. Drain, reserving ¼ cup liquid (add milk if necessary). Place steel blade in work bowl; add drained broccoli, reserved liquid, sour cream, bouillon granules, worcestershire, and garlic salt. Process till smooth, scraping sides of bowl as necessary. Return to saucepan. Heat through; do not boil. Transfer to fondue pot; place over burner. Garnish with parsley, if desired. Serve with bread sticks or crackers. Makes 2½ cups.

Classic Steak Tartare

Serve immediately after making, or chill no longer than 1 hour —

- 1 cup lightly packed parsley (stems removed)
- 1 medium onion, cut into 1-inch pieces
- 1 pound boneless lean beef sirloin or round steak
- 6 egg yolks
  Homemade Horseradish (see recipe, page 76) or prepared horseradish
  Condiments (choose any or all of the following: anchovy fillets, lemon wedges, drained capers, freshly ground pepper, salt, paprika, bottled hot pepper sauce, and worcestershire sauce)
  Buttered toast, cut into quarters

Place steel blade in work bowl; add parsley. Process with on/off turns till finely chopped. Remove from bowl; set aside. Rinse work bowl; reinsert steel blade. Add onion; process with on/off turns till chopped. Remove onion from bowl; set aside.

Trim all gristle and fat from meat; cut meat into 1-inch pieces. Place steel blade in work bowl. Add *half* of the meat; process with on/off turns till finely chopped (refer to illustration for *beef (uncooked) chopped*, page 22). Remove chopped meat from work bowl; repeat steps with remaining meat.

Divide uncooked meat into six portions; shape into mounded patties on chilled plates. Make an indentation in center of each patty; place an uncooked egg yolk in each indentation. Pass the chopped parsley, chopped onion, Homemade Horseradish, and condiments to sprinkle atop and mix into meat and yolk before eating, if desired. Serve with toast. Makes 6 servings.

Quenelles of Pike

Elegant dumplings for a first course or a light supper —

- ¼ cup water
- 1 tablespoon butter or margarine
- ¼ cup all-purpose flour
  Dash salt
- ½ pound fresh or frozen skinless and boneless pike or cod fillets
- 3 tablespoons butter or margarine, cut into pieces
- 1 egg
- 1 egg white
- 1 tablespoon milk
- ¼ teaspoon salt
- ⅛ teaspoon ground nutmeg
  Dash pepper
  Mornay Sauce (see recipe, page 76)

In small saucepan bring water and 1 tablespoon butter or margarine to boiling over medium heat, stirring till butter melts. Add flour and dash salt. Cook and stir over low heat till mixture forms a ball that does not separate. Remove from heat; cool.

Meanwhile, cut fish into 1-inch pieces. Place steel blade in work bowl; add fish and process till smooth. Add the 3 tablespoons butter; process till combined. Add flour mixture, egg, egg white, milk, ¼ teaspoon salt, nutmeg, and pepper. Process till smooth and fluffy. Cover; chill at least 2 hours.

Grease a 10-inch skillet. Using two soup spoons, mold a scant 2 tablespoons fish mixture into an oval shape; gently place in skillet. Repeat with remaining fish mixture.

Combine 2 cups *hot water* and ½ teaspoon *salt*; gently pour down side of skillet. Bring just to boiling. Cover; simmer very gently for 12 to 15 minutes or till quenelles are set. Remove from skillet with slotted spoon; drain on paper toweling. Serve immediately with Mornay Sauce. Makes 16 to 18.

Salmon Dip

Shown on page 44 —

- 1 8-ounce can water chestnuts, drained
- ½ cup lightly packed parsley (stems removed)
- 1 16-ounce can salmon, drained and flaked with skin and bones removed
- 1 8-ounce package cream cheese, quartered
- 2 green onions, cut up
- ¼ cup milk
- 1 tablespoon lemon juice
- 1 teaspoon Homemade Horseradish (see recipe, page 76) or prepared horseradish
- ¼ teaspoon salt
  Assorted crackers and vegetable dippers

Place steel blade in work bowl. Add water chestnuts and parsley; process with on/off turns till coarsely chopped. Remove from bowl. Reinsert steel blade; add salmon, cream cheese, green onions, milk, lemon juice, Homemade Horseradish, and salt. Process till blended, stopping to scrape bowl. Add water chestnuts and parsley; process just till mixed. Cover; chill. Serve with crackers and vegetables. Makes about 3 cups.

Horseradish Spread

- 1 8-ounce package cream cheese, quartered
- 2 to 3 tablespoons Homemade Horseradish (see recipe, page 76) or prepared horseradish
- 2 tablespoons milk

Place steel blade in work bowl; add the cream cheese. Process till smooth. Add the Homemade Horseradish and milk; process just till blended. Makes about 1 cup.

Three-Cheese Spread

½ small onion, quartered
6 ounces cheddar cheese, cubed
1 8-ounce package cream cheese, quartered
2 ounces blue cheese, cubed
2 tablespoons milk
1 tablespoon worcestershire sauce
 Few drops bottled hot pepper sauce
 Assorted crackers

Place steel blade in work bowl. Add onion; process with on/off turns till finely chopped. Add cheddar cheese; process till crumbly. Add rest of ingredients except crackers; process till well blended, scraping bowl as needed. Turn into a 2½-cup mold or bowl. Cover; chill several hours. Unmold; serve with crackers. Makes 2¼ cups.

Gruyère-Apple Spread

¼ cup pecans
1 medium apple, halved
1 8-ounce package cream cheese, quartered
4 ounces gruyère cheese or monterey jack cheese, cubed
1 tablespoon milk
2 teaspoons prepared mustard
2 to 6 chives, cut up
4 Assorted crackers

Place steel blade in work bowl; add pecans. Process with on/off turns till chopped. Remove; set aside.

Insert shredding disk. Peel and core apple; shred. Add to pecans.

Reinsert steel blade; add cream cheese, gruyère or monterey jack cheese, milk, mustard, and chives. Process till creamy. Add pecans and apple; process with on/off turns till mixed. Cover; chill. Serve with crackers. Makes 2 cups.

Chinese Egg Rolls

Shown on page 4 —

 Homemade Egg Roll Skins
1 medium carrot
2 stalks bok choy, cut up
1 cup fresh mushrooms
2 stalks celery, cut up
1 small onion, cut up
8 canned water chestnuts
1 ½-inch piece gingerroot, peeled
8 ounces lean pork, cubed
4 ounces fresh or frozen shrimp, shelled and deveined
1 tablespoon cooking oil
1 egg
2 tablespoons soy sauce
1 tablespoon dry sherry
½ teaspoon sugar
½ teaspoon salt
1 beaten egg
 Cooking oil or shortening for deep-fat frying

Prepare Homemade Egg Roll Skins. Layer between waxed paper. Cover; chill. Insert shredding disk; shred carrot. Transfer to mixing bowl.

Place steel blade in work bowl. Add bok choy and mushrooms; process till finely chopped. Add to carrots. Reinsert steel blade. Add next 4 ingredients; process till finely chopped. Add to carrots.

Reinsert steel blade in work bowl. Add pork and shrimp; process till coarsely chopped. Preheat wok or skillet; add 1 tablespoon oil. Stir-fry pork and shrimp till browned. Add vegetables; stir-fry 2 to 3 minutes. Combine 1 egg, soy, sherry, sugar, and salt. Stir in pork mixture; cool.

Spoon 1½ tablespoons pork mixture onto each Homemade Egg Roll Skin; fold bottom edge up and sides in. Brush top of skin with beaten egg; overlap. Seal. Place, seam down, on waxed paper. Cover with damp cloth. Fry, 2 or 3 at a time, in deep hot oil (365°) for 2 to 3 minutes. Drain. Makes 24 egg rolls.

Homemade Egg Roll Skins

6 eggs
2 cups all-purpose flour
2 cups water
1 teaspoon salt

Place steel blade in work bowl. Add 3 of the eggs, 1 cup flour, 1 cup water, and ½ teaspoon salt. Process till smooth; pour into mixing bowl. Repeat. Heat a lightly greased 6-inch skillet. Remove from heat; add 2 tablespoons batter. Lift and tilt skillet to spread batter evenly. Return to heat; cook 1 minute on one side only (skins will not brown). Invert onto paper toweling. Repeat with remaining batter, greasing skillet occasionally. Makes 24.

Ham-Zucchini Wedges

½ cup lightly packed parsley (stems removed)
3 beaten eggs
4 ounces fully cooked ham, cut into 1-inch pieces
1 small onion
2 ounces Swiss cheese
1 medium zucchini

Place steel blade in work bowl; add parsley. Process with on/off turns till finely chopped; add to beaten eggs. Reinsert steel blade; add ham. Process till finely chopped; add to eggs. Reinsert steel blade. Add onion; chop. Place in saucepan.

Insert shredding disk. Shred cheese; add to egg-ham mixture. Reinsert shredding disk. Shred zucchini; add to onion. Add enough water to cover vegetables. Simmer, covered, 3 minutes or just till tender. Drain well, pressing out excess liquid. Add to egg mixture; mix lightly. Turn into a greased 9-inch pie plate. Bake in 350° oven about 20 minutes or till set. Makes 10 to 12 servings.

Curried Cheese Spread

- 1 stalk celery
- 1 green onion
- ½ medium green pepper
- ½ cup pimiento-stuffed olives
- 1 cup dairy sour cream
- 2 3-ounce packages cream cheese, quartered
- 1 tablespoon lemon juice
- 2 teaspoons curry powder
- ½ teaspoon salt
- ½ teaspoon worcestershire sauce
  Dash bottled hot pepper sauce
  Assorted crackers

Cut celery, green onion, and green pepper into 1-inch pieces. Place steel blade in work bowl; add celery and green onion. Process with on/off turns till coarsely chopped. Add green pepper and olives; process with on/off turns till finely chopped. Add remaining ingredients except crackers; process just till thoroughly blended, stopping to scrape bowl.

Line a 3-cup mold or bowl with clear plastic wrap; spoon in the cheese mixture. Cover and chill overnight. Unmold onto serving plate; remove wrap. Serve with assorted crackers. Makes 2½ cups.

Chive-Cheese Butter

- ⅓ cup lightly packed chives, cut into 1-inch lengths
- 1 ounce parmesan cheese, cubed (¼ cup grated)
- ½ cup butter, cut up

Place steel blade in work bowl; add chives. With machine running, add parmesan through feed tube; process till chives and parmesan are very finely chopped. Add butter; process till mixture is smooth and fluffy. Serve with asparagus, green beans, or corn. Makes ¾ cup.

Lemon-Chive Butter

- ¼ cup lightly packed chives, cut into 1-inch lengths
- 3 1-inch strips lemon peel (cut with vegetable peeler)
- 1 cup butter or margarine, cut into pieces
- 1 tablespoon lemon juice
- ¼ teaspoon pepper

Place steel blade in work bowl; add chives and lemon peel. Process with on/off turns till chopped. Add remaining ingredients; process till smooth. Serve with vegetables, steaks, or fish. Or, melt and use as dip for artichokes or seafood. Makes about 1 cup.

Chili Con Queso

Add a little milk if dip becomes thick —

- 1 medium onion, quartered
- 1 tablespoon butter or margarine
- 1 4-ounce can green chili peppers, rinsed and seeded
- 2 medium tomatoes, peeled
- ¼ teaspoon salt
- 4 ounces cheddar cheese
- 4 ounces process monterey jack cheese food, chilled (5 or 6) slices
  Tortilla chips or corn chips

Insert steel blade; add onion. Process till chopped. Heat butter in 1-quart saucepan. Add onion; cook till tender.

Reinsert steel blade; add chili peppers. Process till coarsely chopped. Add tomatoes; process with 1 or 2 on/off turns till coarsely chopped. Stir into onion; add salt. Simmer for 12 minutes.

Insert shredding disk. Shred the cheeses, folding slices in half. Slowly add to tomato mixture, stirring just till melted. Heat over low heat. Transfer to small fondue pot; place over fondue burner. Serve with chips. Makes 1¾ cups.

Hot Mexican Bean Dip

- 1 16-ounce can refried beans
- 1 4-ounce can green chili peppers, rinsed and seeded
- 2 ounces American cheese, cut into 1-inch pieces
- ½ small onion, quartered
- 1 teaspoon worcestershire sauce
- ½ teaspoon garlic salt
  Few dashes bottled hot pepper sauce (optional)
  Crumbled crisp-cooked bacon
  Tortilla chips

Place steel blade in work bowl; add all ingredients except bacon and chips. Process 30 seconds or till well blended, stopping to scrape bowl. Transfer to small metal fondue pot; place over fondue burner. Top with bacon. Serve with chips. Makes 2 cups.

Beef and Cheese Ball

- 1 cup corn chips (1½ ounces)
- 1 ounce parmesan cheese, cubed (¼ cup grated)
- 1 8-ounce package cream cheese, quartered
- 2 ounces sliced dried or smoked beef
- 2 tablespoons milk
- 1½ teaspoons Homemade Horseradish (see recipe, page 76) or prepared horseradish
  Assorted crackers

Place steel blade in work bowl; add chips. Process till finely crushed; remove and set aside. Reinsert steel blade. With machine running, drop parmesan cheese in feed tube; process till very finely chopped. Add cream cheese, beef, milk, and Homemade or prepared Horseradish. Process till smooth, scraping sides of bowl as needed. Cover; chill. Shape mixture into a ball; roll in crushed chips to coat. Chill. Serve with crackers. Makes one 4½-inch ball.

Herb Butter

2 tablespoons lightly packed parsley (stems removed)
1 tablespoon lightly packed fresh rosemary (stems removed) *or* ½ teaspoon dried rosemary
1 tablespoon lightly packed fresh marjoram (stems removed) *or* ½ teaspoon dried marjoram
½ cup butter *or* margarine, cut into pieces

Place steel blade in work bowl; add parsley, rosemary, and marjoram. Process with on/off turns till very finely chopped. Add butter or margarine; process till smooth and fluffy. Serve with corn on the cob or steaks. Makes ½ cup.

Sunflower-Nut Spread

Shown on page 44 —

¼ cup shelled sunflower seed
1 cup cocktail peanuts
2 tablespoons butter *or* margarine, cut into chunks
1 tablespoon light molasses

Place steel blade in work bowl. Add sunflower seed; process with on/off turns till coarsely chopped. Remove from bowl; set aside. Reinsert steel blade in work bowl; add cocktail peanuts. Process with on/off turns till coarsely chopped. Continue processing till a paste forms.

Add butter and molasses; process till desired thickness. Add chopped sunflower seed; process just till blended. Cover and store in refrigerator. Bring to room temperature for easier spreading. Serve on crackers or as sandwich filling. Makes about 1 cup.

nut butters

Almond

2 cups blanched whole almonds

Before processing, spread in shallow baking pan. Toast in 300° oven for 20 minutes. Cool 5 minutes. (For blanching directions, see page 93.)

Peanut

2 cups cocktail peanuts

(Dry roasted peanuts usually give a more grainy texture.)

Pecan

2 cups pecans

Before processing, toast pecans, if desired. Spread in shallow baking pan; toast in 300° oven for 20 minutes. Cool 5 minutes.

Walnut

2 cups walnuts

(This butter has the darkest color and strongest flavor.)

Place steel blade in work bowl; add nuts. Process till butter forms, stopping to scrape sides of bowl occasionally to make sure all of mixture is evenly blended. This will take 3 to 5 minutes. Continue processing about 2 minutes more or till butter is the desired smoothness. Store in covered container in refrigerator. Bring to room temperature for easier spreading. Makes about 1¼ cups.

For other recipes using nut butters, see pages 41 and 92.

Vegetable-Nut Spread

1 stalk celery, cut up
1 large carrot, cut up
½ cup Nut Butter
1 tablespoon mayonnaise

Insert steel blade. Add celery and carrot; process till finely chopped. Add Nut Butter and mayonnaise; process till blended. Add more mayonnaise, if needed. Chill to store. Makes 1 cup.

Apple-Nut Sandwich Filling

1 small tart apple, peeled, cored, and quartered
½ cup Nut Butter
4 slices bacon, crisp-cooked, drained, and crumbled
2 tablespoons mayonnaise
2 teaspoons lemon juice

Insert steel blade; add apple. Process with 2 or 3 on/off turns till coarsely chopped; add rest of ingredients. Process till blended, but not smooth. Store in refrigerator. Makes 1 cup.

Chicken-Nut Sandwich Filling

1½ cups cut up cooked chicken
½ cup water chestnuts
1 3-ounce package cream cheese with chives, cut up
½ cup Nut Butter
¼ cup milk
¼ cup mayonnaise

Place steel blade in work bowl. Add *1 cup* chicken and water chestnuts. Process with on/off turns till coarsely chopped; remove. Reinsert steel blade. Add ½ cup chicken and rest of ingredients. Process till smooth; stir into chicken-water chestnut mixture. Store in refrigerator. Makes 2 cups.

salads & salad dressings

Sweet Fruit Slaw

- 1 small head cabbage, cored (about 1 pound)
- 1 medium apple, cored and cut into 1-inch pieces
- 1 11-ounce can mandarin orange sections, drained
- ½ cup grapes, halved and seeded
- ¼ cup raisins *or* chopped nuts
- ⅓ cup honey
- 3 tablespoons lemon juice
- 1 teaspoon celery seed, poppy seed, *or* toasted sesame seed
- ½ teaspoon dry mustard
- ½ teaspoon paprika
- ¼ teaspoon salt
- ½ cup salad oil

Insert slicing disk in work bowl. Cut cabbage into wedges to fit feed tube; slice. As work bowl gets full, transfer sliced cabbage to a large bowl (should have about 5 cups).

Place steel blade in work bowl; add apple. Process with on/off turns till chopped. Stir apple, oranges, grapes, and raisins or nuts into cabbage. Cover and chill.

For dressing reinsert steel blade in work bowl; add honey, lemon juice, desired seed, dry mustard, paprika, and salt. Process just till ingredients are mixed. With machine running, gradually pour oil through feed tube in a steady stream (should take about 1 minute). Process about 15 seconds more or till slightly thickened. Transfer to small bowl. Cover and chill.

Just before serving, pour dressing over fruit mixture; toss gently to coat cabbage and fruit. Serve immediately. Makes 10 servings.

24-Hour Cabbage Salad

- 1 medium head cabbage, cored
- 1 medium onion
- 1 small green pepper
- 1½ cups sugar
- 1 cup vinegar
- ½ cup water
- 2 teaspoons salt
- 2 teaspoons mustard seed *or* celery seed
- ¼ cup chopped pimiento

Place steel blade in work bowl. Cut cabbage, onion, and pepper into 1-inch pieces; add 2 *cups* to work bowl. Process with on/off turns till chopped; transfer to large bowl. Reinsert steel blade and repeat with remaining vegetables, processing 2 cups at a time.

Stir together remaining ingredients till sugar dissolves. Pour over cabbage mixture; toss. Cover; chill at least 24 hours. Drain. Serves 12.

Frozen Cranberry Squares

- 3 cups fresh *or* frozen cranberries (12 ounces)
- 3 large apples, cored and cut into 1-inch pieces
- 1 cup sugar
- 1 7-ounce jar marshmallow creme
- 1 cup whipping cream, whipped

Place steel blade in work bowl. Add 1 *cup* of the cranberries; process with on/off turns till very finely chopped. Remove. Reinsert steel blade. Repeat with rest of cranberries and apples; process 1 cup at a time. Stir sugar and marshmallow creme into cranberry mixture. Cover; let stand 3 to 4 hours. Fold whipped cream into cranberry mixture. Turn into a 9x9x2-inch pan. Cover; freeze overnight. Serves 12.

Chicken Stack-Up Salad

- 2 cups cubed cooked chicken
- ¾ teaspoon curry powder
- ¼ teaspoon salt
- ¼ teaspoon paprika
- ⅛ teaspoon pepper
- 1 large green pepper, cut into 1-inch pieces
- 4 ounces cheddar cheese
- 1 medium head lettuce, cored
- 2 small cucumbers
- 1 cup macaroni, cooked and drained
- 1½ cups Homemade Mayonnaise (see recipe, page 55) *or* salad dressing
- 2 tablespoons milk
- 2 tablespoons lemon juice
- ½ teaspoon salt
- Dash pepper
- 1 small tomato, cut into wedges

Place steel blade in work bowl; add chicken. Process with on/off turns till chopped. Transfer chicken to mixing bowl; add curry powder, the ¼ teaspoon salt, paprika, and the ⅛ teaspoon pepper. Toss to coat well; set aside.

Reinsert steel blade; add green pepper. Process with on/off turns till chopped. Remove; set aside.

Insert shredding disk; shred cheese. Remove and set aside. Reinsert shredding disk. Cut lettuce into wedges to fit feed tube; shred lettuce. Transfer to large clear salad bowl. Insert slicing disk; slice cucumbers. In salad bowl layer chicken, cucumber, macaroni, and green pepper atop lettuce.

Stir together Homemade Mayonnaise or salad dressing, milk, lemon juice, ½ teaspoon salt, and dash pepper. Spread over salad mixture. Sprinkle with shredded cheese. Cover; chill several hours or overnight. Garnish with tomato wedges. Makes 8 servings.

Cranberry Relish Salad

Shown on page 4 —

- 1 6-ounce package raspberry-flavored gelatin
- ½ cup sugar
- 3 cups boiling water
- 1 8¼-ounce can crushed pineapple
- 1 tablespoon lemon juice
- 2 stalks celery, cut into 1-inch pieces
- 1 medium apple, cored and cut into 1-inch pieces
- 2 cups fresh or frozen cranberries
- 1 small orange, seeded and cut into 1-inch pieces
- Lettuce

Dissolve gelatin and sugar in boiling water. Stir in *undrained* crushed pineapple and lemon juice. Chill till partially set.

Meanwhile, place steel blade in work bowl. Add celery and apple; process with on/off turns till finely chopped. Transfer to mixing bowl. Reinsert steel blade. Add *1 cup* cranberries; process with on/off turns till finely chopped. Add to apple mixture; repeat with remaining 1 cup cranberries.

Reinsert steel blade in work bowl; add unpeeled orange. Process with on/off turns till finely chopped. Add to apple mixture; mix well. Fold the fruit mixture into partially set gelatin.

Pour into 10 to 12 individual molds or into a 6½-cup mold. Chill till firm. Unmold onto lettuce-lined plate. Makes 10 to 12 servings.

Garden Pasta Salad

- 6 ounces elbow or shell macaroni (about 2 cups)
- ½ cup lightly packed parsley (stems removed)
- 1 small green pepper, cut into 1-inch pieces
- ½ small onion, halved
- 1 medium cucumber
- 2 medium tomatoes, peeled and quartered
- Fresh Herb Dressing
- 4 ounces feta cheese, crumbled

Cook macaroni in a large amount of boiling salted water for 10 to 12 minutes or just till tender; drain. Rinse and set aside.

Place steel blade in work bowl; add parsley. Process with on/off turns till finely chopped. Remove to mixing bowl. Reinsert steel blade; add green pepper and onion. Process with on/off turns till finely chopped; add to parsley.

Reinsert steel blade. Halve cucumber lengthwise; remove seeds. Cut cucumber into 1-inch pieces; add to work bowl. Process with on/off turns till finely chopped; add to parsley. Reinsert steel blade in work bowl; add tomatoes. Process with on/off turns till finely chopped; add to parsley.

Pour Fresh Herb Dressing over vegetables. Toss to combine. Turn drained macaroni into serving bowl. Spoon vegetables with dressing over macaroni. Sprinkle with cheese. Cover; chill thoroughly. Toss to serve. Makes 6 servings.

Fresh Herb Dressing: Place steel blade in work bowl. Add ¼ cup *salad oil*, 3 tablespoons *dry white wine*, 2 tablespoons *lemon juice*, 1 tablespoon *sugar*, 1 tablespoon lightly packed *fresh basil*, (stems removed) or 1 teaspoon *dried basil*, 1 teaspoon *salt*, ¼ teaspoon freshly ground *pepper*, and several dashes bottled *hot pepper sauce*. Process till well blended. Makes about ½ cup.

German Potato Salad

- 8 medium potatoes (2½ pounds)
- 6 slices bacon
- 1 medium onion, cut into 1-inch pieces
- 2 tablespoons all-purpose flour
- 2 tablespoons sugar
- 1½ teaspoons salt
- 1 teaspoon celery seed
- Dash pepper
- 1 cup water
- ⅓ cup vinegar

Place slicing disk in work bowl. Peel potatoes; halve lengthwise if necessary to fit feed tube. Slice potatoes. Cook in boiling salted water for 5 to 7 minutes or till tender; drain.

Meanwhile, cook bacon till crisp; drain, reserving ¼ cup drippings. Crumble bacon; set aside. Place steel blade in work bowl; add onion. Process with on/off turns till chopped; cook onion in reserved drippings till tender. Blend in flour and next 4 ingredients. Add water and vinegar; cook and stir till thickened. Add potatoes and bacon; stir gently to coat. Heat about 5 minutes. Makes 8 to 10 servings.

Russian Dressing

- ⅓ cup catsup
- ¼ cup sugar
- ¼ cup vinegar
- 1 slice of medium onion
- 1 tablespoon worcestershire sauce
- 1 teaspoon dry mustard
- 1 cup salad oil

Place steel blade in work bowl; add first 6 ingredients. Process till well blended and onion is very finely chopped. With machine running, gradually pour oil through feed tube in steady stream; process till desired consistency. Transfer to covered container; chill. Makes 1¾ cups.

Creamy French Dressing

- 1 egg
- ¼ cup vinegar
- 1 tablespoon sugar
- 1 tablespoon paprika
- 1 teaspoon salt
  Dash cayenne
- 1 cup salad oil

Place steel blade in work bowl; add first 6 ingredients. Process just till mixed. With machine running pour oil through feed tube in steady stream. Process about 15 seconds more or till desired consistency. Pour into covered container; chill. Makes 1½ cups.

Thousand Island Dressing

- 1 small stalk celery, cut up
- ¼ medium green pepper, halved
- ¼ small onion, halved
- 1 cup Homemade Mayonnaise *or* salad dressing
- ¼ cup chili sauce
- 1 teaspoon paprika
- ½ teaspoon salt
- 2 hard-cooked eggs, quartered

Place steel blade in work bowl; add celery, green pepper, and onion. Process with on/off turns till finely chopped. Add next 4 ingredients; process just till mixed. Add eggs; process with on/off turns just till chopped. Chill in covered container. Makes 1¾ cups.

Ripe Olive Dressing: Omit celery and pepper; process onion as above. Add Homemade Mayonnaise, chili sauce, ½ teaspoon *celery salt*, ¼ teaspoon *dried basil*, and ¼ teaspoon *worcestershire sauce*; omit paprika and salt. Process till blended. Add ½ cup *pitted ripe olives* and *only* 1 hard-cooked egg; process with on/off turns just till chopped. Chill. Makes 1¾ cups.

Homemade Mayonnaise

Do not try to halve this recipe or the volume will be too small in most processor bowls to ensure formation of the necessary emulsion —

- 2 egg yolks
- 2 tablespoons vinegar
- 2 tablespoons lemon juice
- 1 teaspoon salt
- ½ teaspoon dry mustard
- ¼ teaspoon paprika
  Dash cayenne
- 2 cups salad oil

Place steel blade in work bowl; add first 7 ingredients. Process just till blended. With machine running, quickly add oil through feed tube in a steady stream. Process till desired consistency. Transfer to covered container; chill and use within 1 month. Makes 2 cups.

Lemon-Mustard Dressing

Especially good on spinach salad —

- 1 egg
- 3 cloves garlic, quartered
- 2 1-inch strips lemon peel (cut with vegetable peeler)
- 2 tablespoons lemon juice
- 2 tablespoons milk
- ¾ teaspoon salt
- ½ teaspoon dry mustard
- ½ teaspoon dried thyme
- ¼ teaspoon sugar
- ⅛ teaspoon freshly ground pepper
- 1 cup olive oil *or* salad oil

Place steel blade in work bowl; add all ingredients except the oil. Process till garlic and lemon peel are very finely chopped. With machine running, add oil through feed tube; process till smooth. Pour into covered container; chill. Makes 1⅓ cups.

Blue Cheese Dressing

- 4 ounces blue cheese, cut into pieces
- 1 small onion, quartered
- 1 cup Homemade Mayonnaise *or* salad dressing
- ⅓ cup salad oil
- 2 tablespoons vinegar
- 1 tablespoon sugar
- 1 teaspoon prepared mustard
- ¼ teaspoon salt
- ¼ teaspoon celery seed
  Dash pepper

Place steel blade in work bowl; add blue cheese. Process with on/off turns till crumbled. Remove from bowl; set aside. Reinsert steel blade; add remaining ingredients. Process till smooth. Transfer to covered container; stir in cheese. Cover; chill. Makes 2¼ cups.

Peanut Fruit Dressing

Using dry roasted peanuts usually results in a grainy texture —

- 1 cup cocktail peanuts
- 1 7-ounce jar marshmallow creme
- ½ cup unsweetened pineapple juice
- 2 tablespoons lemon juice

Place steel blade in work bowl; add peanuts. Process with on/off turns till coarsely chopped. Continue processing for 1 to 1½ minutes or till it forms a butter, scraping bowl as needed. Add marshmallow creme. With machine running, pour pineapple juice and lemon juice through feed tube. Process till desired consistency. Transfer to covered container; chill thoroughly (mixture thickens on chilling). Serve on fruit salads. Makes 1⅔ cups.

soups

Creamy Celery-Zucchini Soup

3 green onions, cut into 1-inch pieces, *or* 1 slice onion, quartered
8 stalks celery, cut into 1-inch pieces
1 medium zucchini, halved lengthwise
1 cup water
1 tablespoon instant chicken bouillon granules
¼ teaspoon salt
1½ cups milk
1 tablespoon cornstarch
2 tablespoons butter *or* margarine

Place steel blade in work bowl; add onions. Process with on/off turns till finely chopped. Add *1 cup* of the celery pieces; process with on/off turns till celery is chopped. Transfer vegetables to a 2-quart saucepan. Reinsert steel blade and repeat with remaining celery, processing 1 cup at a time and transferring chopped celery to saucepan.

Insert slicing disk in work bowl; slice zucchini. Add zucchini, water, bouillon granules, and salt to saucepan; bring to boil. Reduce heat; cover and simmer 10 minutes.

Combine milk and cornstarch; stir into vegetable mixture. Cook and stir till thickened and bubbly. Add butter or margarine, stirring to melt. Season to taste with salt and pepper. Makes 4 servings.

Garden Gold Soup,
Creamy Celery-Zucchini Soup,
Borscht

Borscht

3 pounds beef shank crosscuts
2 tablespoons cooking oil
1 medium onion, cut into 1-inch pieces
6 cups water
½ pound carrots, cut into 1-inch pieces (1½ cups)
2 stalks celery, cut into 1-inch pieces (1 cup)
⅓ small head cabbage, cored
1 pound beets without tops, peeled
1 8-ounce can tomato sauce
1 tablespoon lemon juice
2 teaspoons sugar
2 teaspoons salt
⅛ teaspoon pepper
Dairy sour cream

In 4-quart kettle or Dutch oven brown meat in hot oil. Place steel blade in work bowl. Add onion; process with on/off turns till chopped. Add onion and water to kettle with meat. Simmer, covered, about 2 hours or till meat is tender. Reinsert steel blade in work bowl; add about *1 cup* of the carrots. Process till chopped. Transfer to mixing bowl; repeat with remaining carrots. Reinsert steel blade; add celery and process with on/off turns till chopped. Add to carrots.

Insert slicing disk in work bowl. Cut cabbage into wedges to fit feed tube; slice (should yield about 2 cups). Add to vegetables. Insert shredding disk in work bowl; shred beets. Add to vegetables.

When meat is tender, remove from broth; let stand just till cool enough to handle. Cut meat from bones; cut into bite-size pieces. Skim fat from cooking broth. Add meat, vegetables, tomato sauce, lemon juice, sugar, salt, and pepper to broth in kettle. Simmer, covered, about 30 minutes or till vegetables are tender. Serve hot; pass sour cream to top individual servings. Makes 8 servings.

Garden Gold Soup

1 pound carrots (6 medium)
3 medium potatoes, peeled
3 stalks celery with leaves
2 medium onions
2½ teaspoons salt
2 teaspoons instant chicken bouillon granules
¼ teaspoon dried dillweed
¼ teaspoon pepper
2 cups milk
¼ cup butter *or* margarine

Cut up the carrots, potatoes, celery, and onions; place in 3-quart saucepan. Add next 4 ingredients and 4 cups *water*. Simmer, covered, 45 to 60 minutes or till tender. Strain, reserving 2 cups liquid. Place steel blade in work bowl. Add 2 cups of the vegetables; process till smooth. Return to saucepan, repeat with remaining vegetables, processing 2 cups at a time. Return reserved liquid to pan; stir in milk and butter. Cover; heat. Serves 8.

Cabbage-Cheese Soup

4 ounces process Swiss cheese
1 medium carrot
½ small head cabbage, cored
3½ cups milk
1 10¾-ounce can condensed cream of potato soup
½ teaspoon caraway seed

Insert shredding disk in work bowl; shred cheese. Remove. Replace shredding disk; shred carrot. Leave carrot in work bowl; insert slicing disk. Cut cabbage into wedges; slice.

In 3-quart saucepan cook and stir milk and soup till bubbly. Stir in carrot and cabbage. Simmer, covered, 5 minutes or till tender. Stir in cheese, caraway, and ¼ teaspoon *pepper*. Heat and stir till cheese melts. Makes 4 servings.

Lentil-Pepperoni Soup

1 medium onion, quartered
4 ounces pepperoni
1½ cups dry lentils
6 cups water
1 6-ounce can tomato paste
1½ teaspoons salt
¼ teaspoon dried oregano, crushed
¼ teaspoon ground sage
⅛ teaspoon cayenne
1 medium carrot, cut up
1 stalk celery, cut up
2 medium tomatoes, quartered
½ cup bulgur *or* cracked wheat (optional)

Place steel blade in work bowl; add onion. Process with on/off turns till coarsely chopped. Transfer to a 4-quart Dutch oven. Insert slicing disk. Remove and discard inedible casing from pepperoni; slice pepperoni. Add to Dutch oven.

Rinse the lentils. Add lentils, water, tomato paste, salt, oregano, sage, and cayenne to Dutch oven. Bring to boiling. Reduce heat; cover and simmer for 30 minutes.

Meanwhile, place steel blade in work bowl; add the carrot and celery. Process with on/off turns till coarsely chopped. Add the tomatoes. Process with 1 or 2 on/off turns till coarsely chopped. Add vegetables to lentil mixture. Cover and simmer 40 minutes longer or till vegetables are tender.

Cook bulgur according to package directions. Serve soup in individual bowls with mound of cooked bulgur in center. Makes 6 to 8 servings.

Golden Onion Soup

4 ounces Swiss cheese
1½ pounds onions
6 tablespoons butter *or* margarine
¼ cup all-purpose flour
3 10¾-ounce cans condensed chicken broth
¼ cup dry sherry
Salted rye melba toast rounds (optional)

Insert shredding disk; shred cheese. Remove cheese from work bowl; set aside. Insert slicing disk; slice onions.

In 3-quart saucepan melt butter or margarine; add onions. Cover and cook over medium heat about 20 minutes or till tender, stirring occasionally. Sprinkle flour over cooked onions; mix well. Add chicken broth; cook, stirring constantly, till slightly thickened and bubbly. Cook and stir 2 minutes longer. Stir in sherry. Sprinkle some of the shredded cheese atop each serving. Pass toast rounds, if desired. Makes 6 to 8 servings (10 appetizer servings).

Blackberry Soup

1 16-ounce can blackberries
1 8-ounce carton lemon yogurt
⅛ teaspoon ground cinnamon
1 cup water
½ cup grape juice
1 small banana, sliced
2 tablespoons toasted coconut

Place steel blade in work bowl; add the *undrained* berries. Process till smooth; strain into bowl, discarding seeds. Reinsert steel blade; add the strained liquid, yogurt, and cinnamon. Process just till smooth. Pour into bowl; stir in water and grape juice. Cover and chill. Garnish each serving with banana slices and toasted coconut. Makes 6 to 8 servings.

Herbed Tomato Soup

2 medium onions, cut up
¼ cup butter *or* margarine
6 medium tomatoes, quartered
2 cups water
¼ cup lightly packed fresh basil (stems removed) *or* 2 teaspoons dried basil
2 tablespoons lightly packed fresh thyme (stems removed) *or* 1 teaspoon dried thyme
1 tablespoon instant chicken bouillon granules
1 teaspoon salt
⅛ teaspoon pepper

Place steel blade in work bowl; add onions. Process with on/off turns till chopped. In 3-quart saucepan heat butter or margarine. Add onions; cook till tender. Stir in next 5 ingredients; bring to boiling. Reduce heat; cover and simmer 30 to 40 minutes.

Place steel blade in work bowl. Add 2 *cups* of the tomato mixture; process till smooth. Strain, if desired. Repeat with remaining tomato mixture, processing 2 cups at a time. Return all to saucepan. Add salt and pepper; heat through. Makes 4 to 6 servings.

Cantaloupe Mist

1 medium cantaloupe
¼ teaspoon ground cinnamon
1 6-ounce can frozen orange juice concentrate
2 juice cans water (1½ cups)
1 tablespoon lime juice

Place steel blade in work bowl Cut cantaloupe in half; remove seeds. Scoop pulp into work bowl; add cinnamon. Process till smooth. Pour into a large bowl. Reinsert steel blade; add frozen juice concentrate and water. Process till mixed; add to melon mixture. Stir in lime juice. Cover; chill thoroughly. Makes 6 to 8 servings.

Chilled Pea Soup

- ¼ cup lightly packed parsley (stems removed)
- 2 green onions, cut up
- ½ medium head lettuce, cored and cut up
- 2 cups fresh peas *or* 1 10-ounce package frozen peas
- 1 13¾-ounce can chicken broth
- ½ teaspoon salt
- ¼ teaspoon dried thyme
- ¼ teaspoon pepper
- ½ cup whipping cream

Place steel blade in work bowl; add parsley and onion. Process with on/off turns till finely chopped. Add lettuce; process with on/off turns till chopped. Transfer to 2-quart saucepan; add next 5 ingredients. Simmer, covered, 20 minutes. Cool about 15 minutes.

Reinsert steel blade in work bowl; add *half* the soup. Process till smooth; strain. Repeat with remaining soup. Stir in cream. Cover; chill. Makes 4 servings.

Asparagus-Leek Soup

- 4 cups chicken broth
- 3 medium potatoes, peeled and quartered
- 3 medium leeks, cut up
- 1½ pounds fresh asparagus, cut up, *or* 2 8-ounce packages frozen cut asparagus
- 1 teaspoon dried dillweed
- 2 cups light cream

In 3-quart saucepan bring broth to boiling. Add potatoes and leeks. Simmer, covered, 15 minutes. Add asparagus, dillweed, and 1 teaspoon *salt*; simmer, covered, about 10 minutes or till tender.

Place steel blade in work bowl; add *2 cups* of the vegetable mixture. Process till very smooth; remove. Repeat with remaining mixture, processing 2 cups at a time. Return all to saucepan. Stir in cream; heat through. Serves 8.

Vichyssoise

- 1 large leek, cut up
- 2 tablespoons butter
- 3 medium potatoes, peeled
- 2 cups chicken broth
  Dash ground nutmeg
- 1¾ cups light cream
- 1 teaspoon salt

Place steel blade in work bowl; add leek. Process with on/off turns till chopped. In 3-quart saucepan cook leek in butter till tender.

Insert slicing disk. Cut potatoes to fit feed tube; slice. Add to saucepan; add broth and nutmeg. Simmer, covered, 25 to 30 minutes or till potatoes are tender; cool.

Place steel blade in work bowl. Add about *half* of the potato mixture; process 1 to 2 minutes or till smooth. Pour into a bowl; repeat with remaining mixture. Stir in cream, salt, and dash *pepper*. Cover; chill at least 3 hours. Sprinkle with snipped chives, if desired. Makes 8 appetizer servings.

Orange-Apricot Soup

- 2 17-ounce cans unpeeled apricot halves
- 5 1-inch strips orange peel (cut with vegetable peeler)
- ½ cup orange juice
- ¼ teaspoon ground cardamom
- 1 8-ounce carton plain yogurt
- ½ cup milk

Place steel blade in work bowl. Drain apricots, pouring syrup into work bowl; add *half* the apricots, the peel, juice, and cardamom. Process till smooth. Add yogurt and milk; process just till combined. Pour into a bowl. Reinsert steel blade; add remaining apricots. Process with on/off turns till coarsely chopped; stir into soup. Cover; chill. Serves 8 to 10.

Beef-Vegetable Soup

- 1 pound beef stew meat, cut into ½-inch pieces
- 2 tablespoons cooking oil
- 6 cups water
- 1 tablespoon vinegar
- 1½ teaspoons salt
- 1 teaspoon sugar
- ¼ teaspoon pepper
- 1 bay leaf
- 1 small rutabaga, peeled and cut into 1-inch pieces (8 ounces)
- ¼ cup lightly packed parsley (stems removed)
- 2 medium onions, cut into 1-inch pieces
- ½ small head cabbage, cored and cut into wedges
- 2 medium potatoes, peeled and halved
- 2 medium carrots, cut into 3-inch lengths.

In 4½-quart Dutch oven brown *half* the meat at a time in hot oil. Return all meat to Dutch oven; add water, vinegar, salt, sugar, pepper, and bay leaf.

Place steel blade in work bowl; add rutabaga and parsley. Process with on/off turns till coarsely chopped. Add to mixture in Dutch oven. Reinsert steel blade in work bowl; add onions. Process with on/off turns till coarsely chopped. Add to mixture in Dutch oven. Bring to boil. Reduce heat; simmer, covered, 45 to 60 minutes or till meat is nearly tender.

Meanwhile, insert slicing disk in work bowl; slice the cabbage, potatoes, and carrots. Add to Dutch oven. Cover and cook 30 to 40 minutes longer or till vegetables are tender. Remove bay leaf. Makes 6 servings.

vegetables

Stir-Fried Vegetables

- 2 tablespoons cold water
- 2 teaspoons cornstarch
- 2 tablespoons soy sauce
- 1 tablespoon dry sherry
- 2 teaspoons sugar
- ¼ teaspoon salt
  Dash pepper
- 4 stalks celery
- 2 medium zucchini
- 1 medium onion, halved
- 1 large sweet red or green pepper, halved
- 8 ounces fresh mushrooms
- 2 tablespoons cooking oil

In small bowl combine water and cornstarch; stir in soy sauce, dry sherry, sugar, salt, and pepper. Set aside.

Insert slicing disk in work bowl; cut celery in equal lengths about 1-inch shorter than feed tube. Place vertically in feed tube, wedging in last piece of celery; slice. Slice zucchini and onion; transfer vegetables to another bowl. Reinsert slicing disk in work bowl; slice the pepper and mushrooms.

Preheat a wok or large skillet over high heat; add cooking oil. Stir-fry the celery, zucchini, and onion in hot oil for 1 minute. Add the pepper and mushrooms; stir-fry for 3 to 4 minutes or till vegetables are crisp-tender.

Stir the soy mixture; stir into vegetables. Cook, stirring constantly, about 2 minutes or till thickened and bubbly. Serve at once. Makes 6 servings.

Mapled Squash

- 3 pounds butternut squash
- ¼ cup maple or maple-flavored syrup
- 3 tablespoons butter
- ½ teaspoon salt

Halve squash; remove seeds. Place, cut side down, in shallow baking pan; cover with foil. Bake in 350° oven 30 minutes; turn cut side up. Bake, covered, 20 to 30 minutes or till tender. Place steel blade in work bowl; scoop pulp from one squash half into work bowl. Add half each of the syrup, butter, and salt. Process till smooth; turn into 1½-quart casserole. Repeat with rest of squash, syrup, butter, and salt. Bake in 350° oven about 30 minutes. If desired, sprinkle with ground cinnamon or nutmeg and top with more butter. Serves 6.

Sweet Potato Bake

- 6 medium sweet potatoes
- 1 egg
- ¾ cup milk
- 2 tablespoons brown sugar
- 2 tablespoons butter or margarine
- 2 1-inch strips orange peel (cut with vegetable peeler)
- 2 tablespoons orange juice
- ¾ teaspoon salt
- ¼ teaspoon ground cinnamon

In covered pan cook whole sweet potatoes in enough boiling salted water to cover for 30 to 40 minutes or till tender; drain, peel, and quarter.

Place steel blade in work bowl. Add half the potatoes and all of the remaining ingredients; process till smooth. Add remaining potatoes; process till smooth. Turn into greased 1-quart baking dish.

Bake, covered, in 350° oven for 35 to 40 minutes or till heated through. Makes 6 to 8 servings.

Green Beans Supreme

- 1 slice dry bread, broken
- 1 pound fresh green beans
- 1 small onion, quartered
- 3 tablespoons butter or margarine
- 2 tablespoons all-purpose flour
- ½ teaspoon salt
  Dash pepper
- ½ cup milk
- 1 cup dairy sour cream
- 2 ounces American cheese, well chilled

Place steel blade in work bowl; add bread. Process till finely crushed; remove from bowl and set aside.

Insert slicing disk in work bowl. Remove and discard ends from beans. Cut beans to fit width of feed tube; place horizontally in feed tube to within 1 inch of top. Slice; repeat with remaining beans. In covered saucepan cook sliced beans in small amount of boiling salted water 10 to 12 minutes or till crisp-tender. Drain well.

Meanwhile, place steel blade in work bowl; add onion. Process with on/off turns till coarsely chopped. Cook onion in 2 tablespoons of the butter till tender but not brown. Blend in flour, salt, and pepper. Add milk; cook and stir till thickened and bubbly. Place sour cream in bowl; gradually stir in hot mixture. Return to pan. Stir in drained beans; heat and stir till just bubbly. Do not boil. Spoon into 1-quart casserole.

Insert shredding disk; shred cheese. Sprinkle atop bean mixture. Melt the remaining 1 tablespoon butter; toss with reserved crumbs and sprinkle atop cheese. Broil 4 to 5 inches from heat 1 to 2 minutes or till cheese melts and crumbs brown. Makes 6 to 8 servings.

Potato Pancakes

- 4 **slices bacon**
- 1 **small onion, quartered**
- ¼ **cup lightly packed parsley (stems removed)**
- 1 **egg**
- 2 **tablespoons all-purpose flour**
- 1 **teaspoon salt**
- ¼ **teaspoon ground pepper**
- ⅛ **teaspoon ground nutmeg**
- 4 **medium potatoes (1¼ pounds)**
  Shortening

Cook bacon in 10-inch skillet till crisp; drain reserving drippings. Crumble bacon and place in medium mixing bowl.

Place steel blade in work bowl; add onion and parsley. Process with on/off turns till very finely chopped. Add egg, flour, salt, pepper, and nutmeg; process with on/off turns till well mixed. Pour egg mixture into mixing bowl with bacon.

Insert shredding disk in work bowl. Peel potatoes and cut to fit feed tube; shred. Stir into egg mixture. Heat *2 tablespoons* of the reserved bacon drippings in skillet.

For each pancake, spoon ¼ *cup* of the potato mixture into hot drippings; spread slightly to flatten. Cook over medium heat for 2 to 3 minutes on each side or till browned. Drain on paper toweling. Serve immediately. Add additional bacon drippings or shortening as necessary to keep pancakes from sticking. Makes 10.

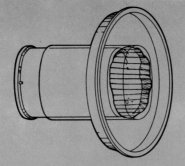

homemade potato rounds or shoestrings

Processors vary in slicing thickness from very thin to quite thick —

- 3 **medium baking potatoes**
- 4 **cups cooking oil**
  Salt

Insert slicing disk in work bowl. Peel potatoes; halve lengthwise, if necessary to fit feed tube.

To make potato rounds: Slice potatoes; fry, a few at a time, as directed below.

To make shoestrings: Slice potatoes; remove from work bowl. Reinsert slicing disk. Turn the cover of the work bowl on its side and pull the pusher out of the feed tube about 2 inches. Insert the cut slices parallel to the sides of the feed tube, as shown above. Wedge in slices snugly so they will not fall out when cover is turned upright. Place cover on bowl; slice potatoes. Fry as directed below.

To fry potatoes: Rinse potato rounds or shoestrings in cold water; pat very dry with paper toweling. In deep heavy saucepan heat oil to 360°. Fry potatoes, a few at a time, for 3 to 7 minutes or till golden (timing depends on thickness). Stir while frying to keep potatoes from sticking together. Drain. Sprinkle with salt. Makes about 4 cups.

Summer Squash Sauté

- 4 **slices bacon**
- 1 **small onion, cut up**
- 4 **small zucchini squash**
- 2 **small yellow crookneck squash**
- 1 **2-ounce jar sliced pimiento**

In 10-inch skillet cook bacon till crisp; drain, reserving 3 tablespoons drippings. Crumble bacon and set aside.

Place steel blade in work bowl; add onion. Process with on/off turns till chopped. Cook onion in reserved drippings till tender. Insert slicing disk. Trim squash, if necessary to fit feed tube; slice. Stir into onion. Sprinkle with 1 teaspoon *salt* and ⅛ teaspoon *pepper*. Cook, covered, over medium-low heat for 10 to 15 minutes; stir occasionally. Drain off liquid. Drain pimiento; add to skillet. Stir in bacon. Cover; heat through. Makes 6 to 8 servings.

Creamy Caraway Cabbage

- 1 **small head cabbage, cored and cut into wedges**
- 1 **large onion, halved**
- 1 **cup dairy sour cream**
- 2 **tablespoons all-purpose flour**
- 1 **tablespoon prepared mustard**
- 1 **teaspoon caraway seed**

Insert slicing disk. Slice cabbage; remove as work bowl fills. Slice onion. In 3-quart saucepan bring ½ cup *water* and ½ teaspoon *salt* to boiling; add cabbage and onion. Cook, covered, 7 to 8 minutes or till crisp-tender; drain, reserving cooking liquid. Add water to make ¾ cup.

Mix rest of ingredients, ½ teaspoon *salt*, and ⅛ teaspoon *pepper*; stir in cooking liquid. Fold in vegetables. Turn into 1½-quart casserole. Bake, covered, in 350° oven 20 to 25 minutes; stir once. Serves 6.

Carrot-Rice Bake

- 1 pound carrots (6 medium)
- 1½ cups water
- ⅔ cup long grain rice
- ½ teaspoon salt
- 8 ounces American cheese, well chilled
- 2 beaten eggs
- 1 cup milk
- 2 tablespoons minced dried onion
- ¼ teaspoon pepper

Insert shredding disk; shred carrots (should yield 3 cups). In saucepan combine carrots, water, rice, and salt. Bring to boiling; reduce heat and simmer, covered, 25 minutes. *Do not drain.*

Meanwhile, reinsert shredding disk; shred cheese. Stir *1½ cups* of cheese into carrot mixture. Stir in eggs, milk, onion, and pepper. Turn into 10x6x2-inch baking dish.

Bake in 350° oven about 30 minutes or till knife inserted off center comes out clean. Top with rest of cheese. Bake 2 minutes more to melt cheese. Serves 8.

Puffy Cheese Noodles

- 2 ounces parmesan cheese, cubed (½ cup grated)
- ¾ cup all-purpose flour
- 1 teaspoon baking powder
- ¼ teaspoon salt
- 1 egg
- 1 tablespoon milk

Place steel blade in *dry* work bowl. Add cheese; process till grated. Add next 4 ingredients; process till consistency of cornmeal. With machine running, slowly pour milk through feed tube; process till moistened. On lightly floured surface form dough into a ball by hand; roll to a 12-inch square. Slice, cut, dry, and cook as in tip, right. Use same day; do not store. Makes 2½ cups (6 ounces).

preparing noodles

Roll up dough loosely. Slice ¼ inch wide; unroll. Cut into desired lengths. Spread out and dry on racks for 2 hours.

If not cooked immediately, store homemade noodles, covered, in the refrigerator to retard molding.

To cook, drop noodles into large amount of boiling salted water or soup. Cook, uncovered, 10 to 12 minutes.

Homemade Noodles

- 1 cup all-purpose flour
- ½ teaspoon salt
- 1 egg
- 2 tablespoons milk

Place steel blade in *dry* work bowl; add flour, salt, and egg. Process till consistency of cornmeal. With machine running, slowly pour milk through feed tube. Process till a ball forms. Transfer to floured surface; cover. Let rest 10 minutes. Roll to 16x12-inch rectangle. Let stand 15 to 20 minutes. Slice, dry, and store or cook as in tip above. Makes 3 cups (7 ounces).

Whole Wheat Noodles: Prepare as directed above, *except* substitute ½ cup *whole wheat flour* for ½ cup of the all-purpose flour.

Green Noodles

Shown on pages 4 and 74 —

- 2½ cups tightly packed torn spinach leaves
- ¼ cup water
- 2 eggs
- 1 teaspoon salt
- 2½ cups all-purpose flour

In covered pan cook spinach in water till very tender (it cooks down to about ½ cup); cool. Place steel blade in work bowl; add *undrained* spinach, eggs, and salt. Process till smooth. Add flour; process till a ball forms.

On floured surface roll *half* of the dough at a time to an 18x15-inch rectangle. Let stand 20 minutes. Slice, cut, dry, and store or cook as in tip, left. Makes 7 cups (1 pound).

Pesto

- 1 ounce romano cheese, cubed
- 2 tablespoons pine nuts, walnuts, *or* almonds
- 1 small clove garlic, quartered
- ⅛ teaspoon salt
- 1 cup lightly packed fresh basil (stems removed)
- ½ cup lightly packed fresh parsley (stems removed)
- 3 tablespoons olive oil *or* cooking oil

Place steel blade in work bowl; add cheese, nuts, garlic, and salt. Process with on/off turns till very finely chopped. Add basil and parsley. Process till a paste forms; scrape bowl as needed. With machine running, slowly add oil through feed tube; process till consistency of soft butter.

Refrigerate or freeze till used. Toss with hot buttered noodles (use about ⅓ cup pesto to about 8 ounces noodles). Or sprinkle atop soups. Makes ⅔ cup.

main dishes

Veal and Zucchini

1 pound veal leg round steak *or* beef round steak, cut ¼ inch thick
2 tablespoons all-purpose flour
1 tablespoon cooking oil
3 to 4 tablespoons water
8 ounces unpeeled zucchini (1 or 2)
4 ounces fresh mushrooms (1½ cups)
1 clove garlic, halved
4 sprigs parsley (stems removed)
1 cup dairy sour cream
⅓ cup milk
1 tablespoon all-purpose flour
1 tablespoon dijon-style mustard
1 tablespoon dry sherry
¼ teaspoon salt

Cut meat into four portions; pound with meat mallet to flatten slightly. Coat with 2 tablespoons flour. In 10-inch skillet brown meat, 2 pieces at a time, in hot oil. Return all meat to skillet; add water. Reduce heat; cover and simmer for 15 minutes.

Meanwhile, place slicing disk in work bowl; slice zucchini and mushrooms. Add to meat; simmer, covered, about 15 minutes longer or till meat is tender. Transfer to platter; keep warm. Place steel blade in work bowl; add garlic and parsley. Process with on/off turns till finely chopped. Add sour cream, milk, the 1 tablespoon flour, mustard, sherry, and salt. Process just till mixed. Pour into skillet; cook and stir over low heat till mixture starts to bubble. *Do not boil.* Spoon over meat and vegetables. Makes 4 servings.

Turkey Loaf with Pineapple-Orange Sauce

2 slices bread, torn
1 medium green pepper, cut up
1 small onion, quartered
½ of an 8-ounce can water chestnuts, drained
1 2½- to 3-pound frozen turkey hindquarter, thawed
2 eggs
1 tablespoon soy sauce
1 teaspoon salt
¼ teaspoon pepper
½ of a 6-ounce can frozen pineapple juice concentrate (about ⅓ cup)
¼ cup orange marmalade
2 tablespoons bottled steak sauce

Place steel blade in work bowl; add bread. Process till finely crumbled; remove and set aside. Reinsert steel blade in work bowl; add green pepper, onion, and water chestnuts. Process till coarsely chopped; add to bread.

Cut turkey meat from bones; discard bones. Cut meat into 1-inch pieces. Place steel blade in work bowl. Add ⅓ of the turkey; process till finely chopped. Remove and set aside. Repeat with second ⅓ of the turkey. Process remaining ⅓ of the turkey; leave in work bowl. Add the bread-vegetable mixture, eggs, soy sauce, salt, and pepper. Process till mixed. Add the rest of the chopped turkey; process just till all ingredients are well mixed.

Pat into 8x4x2-inch loaf pan. Bake in 350° oven 1 hour; drain. Meanwhile, in small saucepan combine frozen juice concentrate, marmalade, and steak sauce; cook and stir till heated through. Brush some sauce over meat. Return to oven; bake 15 minutes more. Let cool in pan 10 minutes. Remove loaf to platter; pass remaining sauce. Makes 6 to 8 servings.

Glazed Ham Balls

⅓ cup lightly packed parsley (stems removed)
1 pound fully cooked ham, cut into 1-inch cubes
½ pound boneless lean beef, cut into 1-inch cubes
1 slice bread, torn
½ cup milk
½ teaspoon dry mustard
¾ cup unsweetened pineapple juice
½ cup maple *or* maple-flavored syrup
2 tablespoons cornstarch
1 teaspoon lemon juice
4 cups hot cooked rice

Place steel blade in work bowl; add parsley. Process with on/off turns till finely chopped. Remove parsley; set aside.

Wipe bowl; reinsert steel blade. Add *half* of the ham; process with on/off turns till chopped. Remove and set aside. Repeat with remaining ham. Reinsert steel blade in work bowl; add beef cubes and torn bread. Process with on/off turns till meat is chopped.

To meat in work bowl add chopped ham, milk, dry mustard, and *half* the parsley. Process till well blended. Shape mixture into twenty 1½-inch meatballs. Place in 8x8x2-inch baking dish. Bake, uncovered, in 350° oven for 20 minutes.

Meanwhile, in small saucepan combine pineapple juice, maple syrup, cornstarch, and lemon juice. Cook and stir till thickened and bubbly; pour over meatballs and bake 20 minutes longer. Toss hot cooked rice with remaining parsley. Arrange meatballs and sauce atop parslied rice on platter. Makes 4 or 5 servings.

Glazed Ham Balls,
Veal and Zucchini

Ham-Egg Crepes

½　medium onion, quartered
2　cups fresh mushrooms
¼　cup butter *or* margarine
4　ounces American cheese
¼　cup all-purpose four
2　teaspoons prepared mustard
2　cups milk
⅓　cup dairy sour cream
12　ounces fully cooked ham, cut
　　into 1-inch pieces
4　hard-cooked eggs, quartered
16　Crepes

Place steel blade in work bowl; add onion. Process with on/off turns till finely chopped. Remove steel blade, leaving onion in bowl. Insert slicing disk, slice mushrooms.

For sauce, in saucepan cook onion and mushrooms in butter or margarine till tender. Meanwhile, insert shredding disk; shred cheese and set aside. Blend flour and mustard into onion mixture. Add milk. Cook and stir till mixture thickens and bubbles. Stir in cheese till melted. Remove from heat; stir ⅔ *cup* of the cheese mixture into sour cream.

Place steel blade in work bowl; add *half* the meat. Process with on/off turns till finely chopped. Stir into sour cream mixture. Repeat with rest of meat. Season with salt. Reinsert steel blade; add eggs. Process with on/off turns till chopped; add to meat mixture.

Spoon a scant ¼ cup meat mixture onto center of each crepe. Roll up; place, seam side down, in 13x9x2-inch baking dish. Pour remaining ⅓ cup cheese mixture over crepes. Bake in 375° oven 20 to 25 minutes or till heated through. Makes 8 servings.

To make-ahead: Place filled crepes in baking dish; do not add sauce. Cover crepes and sauce separately; chill up to 24 hours. To serve, stir sauce; pour over crepes. Bake in 375° oven about 30 minutes.

freezing crepes

Unfilled crepes freeze well. Just make a stack, alternating each crepe with two layers of waxed paper. (The waxed paper makes crepes easy to separate.) Then, overwrap the stack in a moisture-vapor-proof bag. Before freezing, protect crepes by placing bag in a glass or plastic container. Use crepes within 4 months, removing as many as needed and resealing the bag. Let crepes thaw at room temperature about 1 hour before using.

Crepes

If your machine has a plastic blade, use it for mixing the batter —

2　eggs
1½　cups milk
1　cup all-purpose flour
1　tablespoon cooking oil
¼　teaspoon salt

Place steel blade in work bowl; add eggs, milk, flour, cooking oil, and salt. Process about 15 seconds or till smooth. Lightly grease a 6-inch skillet; heat. Pour 2 tablespoons batter into skillet; lift and tilt pan from side to side till batter covers bottom. Return to heat; brown one side only. Invert onto paper toweling. Repeat with remaining batter. Makes 16 crepes.

Whole Wheat Crepes: Prepare as above, substituting 1 cup *whole wheat flour* for the all-purpose flour.

Leek Quiche

The white portion of the leek is more tender than the green portion —

1　unbaked 9-inch pastry shell
8　slices bacon
2　large leeks
8　ounces Swiss cheese
3　eggs
1½　cups milk
1　tablespoon all-purpose flour
½　teaspoon salt
　　Dash ground nutmeg

 Bake the unpricked pastry shell in 425° oven about 6 minutes or just till lightly browned. (Pastry may puff but will settle.) Remove from oven; reduce temperature to 325°.

In skillet cook bacon till crisp; drain, reserving 2 tablespoons drippings in skillet. Crumble bacon; set aside 2 tablespoons. Sprinkle remaining in pastry shell.

Insert slicing disk in work bowl; slice leeks (should have about 2 cups). Cook leeks in reserved drippings about 5 minutes or till tender but not brown; drain.

Meanwhile, insert shredding disk in work bowl; shred cheese. Sprinkle cheese and leeks atop bacon in pastry shell. Place steel blade in work bowl; add eggs, milk, flour, salt, and nutmeg. Process till blended. Pour mixture into pastry shell. Sprinkle with reserved bacon.

Bake in 325° oven about 45 minutes or till nearly set in center. Let stand 10 to 15 minutes before serving. Makes 6 servings.

Ham-Egg Crepes, Moussaka
(see recipe, page 68)

Moussaka

Shown on page 67 —

- 1 slice bread
- 2 ounces American cheese
- 2 medium eggplants, peeled (2 pounds)
- 2 medium onions, quartered
- 8 sprigs parsley (stems removed)
- 1 pound boneless beef chuck, gristle and excess fat removed
- ¼ cup dry red wine
- ¼ cup water
- 1 tablespoon tomato paste
- 1 teaspoon salt
  Dash pepper
- 2 eggs
- ¼ teaspoon ground cinnamon
- 3 tablespoons butter *or* margarine
- 3 tablespoons all-purpose flour
- ½ teaspoon salt
- ⅛ teaspoon ground nutmeg
  Dash pepper
- 1½ cups milk
- 1 beaten egg
  Cooking oil

Insert shredding disk in work bowl. Fold the slice of bread in half; shred. Remove and set aside. Shred cheese; remove and set aside. Insert the slicing disk in work bowl. Cut eggplants into pieces to fit feed tube; slice. Transfer to another dish; sprinkle with a little salt and set aside.

Place steel blade in work bowl. Add onions and parsley; process till coarsely chopped. Remove and set aside. Reinsert steel blade in work bowl. Cut meat into 1-inch pieces; add *half* of the meat to work bowl. Process with on/off turns till chopped; transfer to large skillet. Repeat with remaining meat; add to skillet. Add onion mixture. Cook till browned; drain off excess fat.

Stir in wine, water, tomato paste, 1 teaspoon salt, and dash pepper.

Simmer about 4 minutes or till liquid is nearly evaporated; cool slightly. Stir in *half* of the bread, half the cheese, 2 eggs, and the cinnamon; set aside.

For sauce, in saucepan melt the butter or margarine; stir in flour, ½ teaspoon salt, nutmeg, and dash pepper. Add milk all at once; cook and stir till thickened and bubbly. Stir *half* of the hot mixture into the 1 beaten egg; return all to saucepan. Cook and stir over low heat 2 minutes; set aside.

Brown eggplant slices in a little hot oil. Sprinkle bottom of a 12x7½x2-inch baking dish with remaining bread. Cover with half the eggplant; spoon on the meat mixture. Arrange remaining eggplant slices atop; pour sauce over all. Bake, uncovered, in 350° oven about 45 minutes or till set. Sprinkle with remaining cheese. Bake 2 to 3 minutes longer to melt cheese. Makes 6 to 8 servings.

Parmesan Chicken

- 3 ounces parmesan cheese cut up (¾ cup grated)
- 2 slices dry bread, broken up
- ¼ cup lightly packed parsley (stems removed)
- 1 2½ to 3-pound broiler-fryer chicken, cut up
- ¼ cup butter *or* margarine, melted

Place steel blade in work bowl. Add cut-up parmesan; process till coarsely chopped. Add dried bread and parsley; process till all are finely chopped. Transfer to shallow dish.

Brush chicken pieces with melted butter; roll in cheese mixture. Place chicken, skin side up, in shallow baking pan. Drizzle remaining butter atop; sprinkle on remaining cheese mixture. Bake in 375° oven for 45 to 60 minutes or till tender; do not turn. Makes 4 servings.

Beef Tacos

Heat taco shells while preparing meat mixture, if desired. Arrange shells on baking sheet lined with paper toweling; warm in 250° oven —

- 4 ounces sharp cheddar cheese
- 1 small head lettuce, cored
- 2 medium tomatoes, quartered
- 1 medium onion, quartered
- 1 clove garlic
- 1 pound boneless beef chuck, gristle and excess fat removed
- 1 to 2 teaspoons chili powder
- ¾ teaspoon salt
- 12 packaged taco shells
  Bottled taco sauce

Insert shredding disk in work bowl; shred cheddar cheese. Remove and set aside. Insert slicing disk in work bowl. Cut lettuce into wedges to fit feed tube; slice lettuce. Remove and set aside.

Place steel blade in work bowl; add tomatoes. Process with 1 or 2 on/off turns just till chopped. Remove and set aside. Reinsert steel blade in work bowl; add onion and garlic. Process till chopped; remove to skillet.

Reinsert steel blade in work bowl. Cut the meat into 1-inch pieces. Place *half* of the meat in work bowl; process till chopped. Add to onion mixture in skillet. Repeat with remaining meat.

Cook meat, onion, and garlic till meat is brown and onion is tender; drain off fat. Season with chili powder and salt. Fill each taco shell with some of the meat mixture, tomatoes, lettuce, and cheese. Pass bottled taco sauce to drizzle atop. Makes 6 servings.

Stuffed Steak

If you don't have an oven-going skillet transfer the browned steaks to a 12x7½x2-inch baking dish —

- 2 tablespoons all-purpose flour
- ½ teaspoon salt
- ¼ teaspoon garlic salt
- ⅛ teaspoon pepper
- 2 pounds beef round steak, cut ½ inch thick
- 8 canned water chestnuts
- 3 green onions, cut into 1-inch pieces
- 1 cup fresh mushrooms
- 2 medium carrots
- 2 tablespoons shortening
- ⅔ cup dry red wine

Combine flour, salt, garlic salt, and pepper; sprinkle on meat. Pound with meat mallet till meat is about ¼ inch thick. Cut meat into 6 pieces.

Place steel blade in work bowl; add water chestnuts and green onions. Process with on/off turns till coarsely chopped; spoon vegetables over each piece of meat. Reinsert steel blade. Add mushrooms to work bowl; process with on/off turns till coarsely chopped; spoon over meat.

Insert shredding disk in work bowl; shred carrot. Spoon some shredded carrot over each piece of meat. Sprinkle generously with salt. Roll up each piece of meat, starting from shortest side. Tie or skewer to secure.

In 10-inch oven-going skillet brown meat slowly on all sides in hot shortening. Pour wine over meat. Cover and bake in 350° oven for 45 minutes. Uncover; bake 15 minutes more or till tender. Pass juices with meat. Makes 6 servings.

Skillet Pork Chops and Hot Slaw

Shown on page 5 —

- 4 pork chops, cut ½ inch thick (1½ to 2 pounds)
- 2 tablespoons cooking oil
- 2 tablespoons water
- ½ medium head cabbage, cored
- 2 medium carrots
- 1 medium onion, cut into 1-inch pieces
- 1 medium green pepper, cut into 1-inch pieces
- ¼ cup vinegar
- ¼ cup water
- 1 tablespoon all-purpose flour
- 1 tablespoon sugar
- 1 tablespoon prepared mustard
- 2 teaspoons worcestershire sauce
- 1 teaspoon salt
- ½ teaspoon celery seed

In a 10-inch skillet slowly brown chops on both sides in hot oil, allowing about 10 minutes total time. Season with a little salt and pepper. Add 2 tablespoons water; cover. Simmer 20 to 25 minutes.

Meanwhile, insert slicing disk in work bowl. Cut cabbage into wedges to fit feed tube; slice. Transfer to mixing bowl. Insert shredding disk; shred carrots. Add to cabbage. Place steel blade in work bowl. Add onion and green pepper; process with on/off turns till chopped. Add to cabbage mixture. Reinsert steel blade in work bowl. Add vinegar, ¼ cup water, flour, sugar, mustard, worcestershire sauce, salt, and celery seed; process till smooth.

When chops are tender, remove from skillet; keep warm. Stir vinegar mixture into pan drippings; cook and stir till thickened. Add vegetables, stirring to coat with vinegar; top with chops. Simmer, covered, 5 minutes more. Makes 4 servings.

Pork Steaks with Apple Stuffing

- 6 pork shoulder blade steaks, cut ½ inch thick (about 3¾ pounds)
- 2 tablespoons shortening
- 2 large apples, cored and cut into 1-inch pieces
- 1 stalk celery, cut into 1-inch pieces
- 1 medium onion, cut into 1-inch pieces
- 3 cups plain croutons
- ½ cup raisins
- ¾ teaspoon salt
- ½ teaspoon poultry seasoning
  Dash pepper
- 1 teaspoon instant beef bouillon granules
- ⅓ cup hot apple juice or water

In large skillet slowly brown 3 of the steaks on both sides in hot shortening. Season generously with salt and pepper. Place in a 15x10x1-inch baking pan. Repeat with remaining steaks.

Place steel blade in work bowl; add apple. Process with on/off turns till finely chopped. Remove apple to mixing bowl; reinsert steel blade in work bowl. Add celery and onion; process with on/off turns till finely chopped. Add to apple. Add croutons, raisins, salt, poultry seasoning, and pepper.

Dissolve bouillon granules in hot apple juice or water; toss with apple mixture. Spoon onto steaks, pressing lightly. Cover; bake in 350° oven about 45 minutes. Uncover and bake 10 minutes more. Makes 6 servings.

breads

Pizza Batter Bread

2 ounces pepperoni, casing removed and cut into ½-inch pieces
3 cups all-purpose flour
1 package active dry yeast
½ teaspoon dried oregano
¼ teaspoon garlic powder
1¼ cups water
2 tablespoons butter *or* margarine
1 tablespoon sugar
1 teaspoon salt

Place steel blade in work bowl. With machine running drop pepperoni pieces through feed tube; process till finely chopped. Add 1½ *cups* of the flour, the yeast, oregano, and garlic powder; process with on/off turns till mixed.

In saucepan heat water, butter or margarine, sugar, and salt just till warm (115° to 120°) and butter is almost melted; stir constantly. Pour into measuring cup or small pitcher. With machine running pour mixture through feed tube. Stop machine; add the remaining 1½ cups flour and process with 4 on/off turns. Turn on again and process 5 to 10 seconds longer or till well mixed.

Transfer to greased bowl. Cover and let rise in warm place till double (45 to 60 minutes). Stir dough down. Spread evenly in greased 9x5x3-inch loaf pan. Cover; let rise till double (about 30 minutes). Bake in 375° oven for 35 to 40 minutes or till done. Remove from pan; cool on rack. Makes 1 loaf.

Carrot-Bran Muffins

1¼ cups whole bran cereal
1 cup buttermilk
2 medium carrots, cut up
1 egg
3 tablespoons cooking oil
1 cup all-purpose flour
¼ cup packed brown sugar
2 teaspoons baking powder
½ teaspoon baking soda

Mix bran and buttermilk; let stand 3 minutes. Insert steel blade; add carrots. Process till chopped. Add egg, oil, and bran mixture. Process till mixed. Add mixture of flour, rest of ingredients, and ½ teaspoon *salt*. Process with 2 or 3 on/off turns; *do not overmix*. (Batter is thick.) Fill greased muffin pans ⅔ full. Bake in 400° oven 20 minutes. Makes 12 to 14.

Zucchini Nut Loaf

½ cup walnuts
1 1-inch strip lemon peel (cut with vegetable peeler)
1 medium unpeeled zucchini
1 egg
½ cup cooking oil
1½ cups all-purpose flour
¾ cup sugar
1 teaspoon ground cinnamon
½ teaspoon salt
½ teaspoon baking soda
½ teaspoon ground nutmeg
¼ teaspoon baking powder

Insert steel blade; add nuts and peel. Process till chopped; remove. Insert shredding disk. Shred zucchini (to make 1 cup); remove. Reinsert steel blade; add zucchini, egg, and oil. Process till mixed. Add mixture of flour, rest of ingredients, nuts, and peel. Process with 3 or 4 on/off turns; *do not overmix*. Turn into greased 8x4x2-inch loaf pan. Bake in 325° oven 60 to 65 minutes. Cool in pan 10 minutes; remove. Cool. Makes 1.

Orange-Date Nut Bread

1 medium orange
1 cup walnuts
1 cup pitted dates, halved
2 cups all-purpose flour
1 egg
½ cup water
2 tablespoons butter *or* margarine, melted
½ cup sugar
2 teaspoons baking powder
½ teaspoon baking soda
½ teaspoon salt

Use vegetable peeler to cut strips of outer portion of peel from orange; cut peel into 1-inch pieces. Cut off white membrane from orange; discard. Quarter orange, discarding seeds. Place steel blade in work bowl; add peel, walnuts, dates, and ¼ *cup* of the flour. Process with on/off turns till chopped. Remove from bowl; set aside. Reinsert steel blade in work bowl. Add quartered orange, egg, water, and melted butter or margarine; process till nearly smooth.

Stir together remaining 1¾ cups flour, sugar, baking powder, soda, salt, and date mixture; add to work bowl. Process with on/off turns just till flour disappears. *Do not overmix*. Turn into 3 greased 6x3x2-inch loaf pans *or* one 8x4x2-inch loaf pan.

Bake in 350° oven for 35 to 40 minutes for the small loaves *or* 55 to 60 minutes for the large loaf. Cool in pans 10 minutes; remove to wire rack. Cool thoroughly. If desired, wrap and store overnight. Makes 3 small or 1 large loaf.

Pizza Batter Bread
Orange-Date Nut Bread
Carrot-Bran Muffins

Swiss Rye Bread

- 3 ounces Swiss cheese
- 1 cup milk
- 1 tablespoon sugar
- ¾ teaspoon salt
- 1 package active dry yeast
- 1¾ cups all-purpose flour
- ¾ cup rye flour

Insert shredding disk in work bowl; shred cheese. Remove and set aside.

In saucepan heat milk, sugar, and salt over medium-low heat just till mixture is lukewarm (110°), stirring constantly. Stir in yeast; let stand 5 minutes.

Place steel blade in work bowl; add the all-purpose and rye flours, shredded cheese, and *half* of the milk-yeast mixture. Process with 4 on/off turns. Add remaining milk-yeast mixture; process with 4 on/off turns. Turn machine on again and process about 15 seconds or till ball of dough forms. *Do not process more than 60 seconds.* (If dough seems sticky to the touch, add 1 to 2 tablespoons additional all-purpose flour; process with 1 or 2 on/off turns.)

Place ball of dough in lightly greased bowl; turn once to grease surface. Cover; let rise in warm place till double (45 to 60 minutes). Punch down. Cover; let rest 10 minutes. Shape into a loaf. Place in greased 8x4x2-inch loaf pan. Cover and let rise till nearly double (30 to 45 minutes).

Bake in 375° oven for 35 to 40 minutes or till done. If top of bread browns too quickly, cover loosely with foil the last 15 to 20 minutes. Makes 1 loaf.

White Bread

For more information on making yeast breads, see page 39 —

- 1 package active dry yeast
- 1 cup warm milk (110° to 115°)
- 3 cups all-purpose flour
- 1 tablespoon sugar
- 1 teaspoon salt
- 1 tablespoon cooking oil

Soften yeast in warm milk; set aside. Place steel blade in work bowl; add *2 cups* of the flour, the sugar, and salt. Add *half* of the milk-yeast mixture; process with 4 on/off turns. Add remaining milk-yeast mixture and oil; process with 4 on/off turns.

Add remaining 1 cup flour; process with 4 on/off turns. Turn machine on again and process about 15 seconds or till ball of dough forms. *Do not process more than 60 seconds.* (If dough seems sticky to the touch, add 2 to 3 tablespoons additional flour; process with 1 or 2 on/off turns.)

Place ball of dough in lightly greased bowl; turn once to grease surface. Cover; let rise in warm place till double (1 to 1¼ hours). Punch down. Cover; let rest 10 minutes. Shape into a loaf. Place in greased 8x4x2-inch loaf pan. Cover and let rise in warm place till double (about 45 minutes).

Bake in 375° oven 40 to 45 minutes or till done. If bread browns too quickly, cover loosely with foil the last 15 minutes. Remove from pan; cool on wire rack. Makes 1 loaf.

Easy-Mix Method: Use ingredients as above. Place steel blade in work bowl; add *2 cups* of the flour, the yeast, sugar, and salt. Process with 4 on/off turns. Add *half* of the milk; process with 4 on/off turns. Add remaining milk and oil; process with 4 on/off turns. Add remaining 1 cup flour; continue as above.

Cheese Batter Bread

- ¼ cup lightly packed parsley (stems removed)
- 2 ounces parmesan cheese, cut up (½ cup grated)
- 2¼ cups all-purpose flour
- 1 package active dry yeast
- ¾ cup cream-style cottage cheese
- ½ cup water
- 2 tablespoons butter *or* margarine
- 1 egg

Place steel blade in work bowl. Add parsley; process till chopped. Add parmesan; process till parsley and parmesan are finely chopped. Add *1¼ cups* of the flour and the yeast. Process with on/off turns till combined.

In saucepan heat together the cottage cheese, water, and butter or margarine just till warm (115° to 120°) and butter is almost melted, stirring constantly.

With machine running pour heated mixture through feed tube; add egg. Stop machine; add remaining 1 cup flour. Process with 4 on/off turns; continue processing for 5 to 10 seconds or till well mixed (dough does not form a ball). Turn dough into greased bowl. Cover; let rise till double (45 to 60 minutes). Stir down. Spread evenly in a greased 1½-quart casserole. Cover; let rise till nearly double (about 45 minutes). Bake in 350° oven for 45 to 55 minutes. If top of bread browns too quickly, cover loosely with foil the last 15 minutes. Remove from casserole; cool. Makes 1 round loaf.

Brioche Loaf

Brushing with egg yolk-and-milk mixture gives the loaf a golden color. Use either a standard loaf pan or a special brioche mold —

- 1 package active dry yeast
- ¼ cup warm water (110° to 115°)
- 2¼ cups all-purpose flour
- 6 tablespoons cold butter, cut into pieces
- 4 teaspoons sugar
- ½ teaspoon salt
- 2 eggs
- 1 egg yolk
- 1 tablespoon milk

Soften yeast in the warm water. Place steel blade in work bowl; add flour, butter, sugar, and salt. Process till butter is very finely cut into flour mixture. Add yeast-water mixture and eggs; process about 20 seconds or till mixture forms a dough. *Do not process more than 60 seconds.*

(If dough seems sticky, add about 1 tablespoon additional flour; process with 1 or 2 on/off turns.) Place in a lightly greased bowl, turning once to grease surface. Cover and let rise in warm place till double (about 1½ hours). Punch down; cover and let rest 10 minutes.

Shape into a loaf and place in greased 8x4x2-inch loaf pan. *Or,* shape into a ball and place in greased 6-cup brioche mold. Cover; let rise till double (about 1 hour). If desired, combine the egg yolk and milk; brush over loaf. Bake in 350° oven about 30 minutes or till done. Remove from pan; cool on rack. Makes 1 loaf.

Almond Coffee Cake

- ¾ cup milk
- 6 tablespoons butter
- 3 cups all-purpose flour
- 1 package active dry yeast
- ⅓ cup sugar
- 1 egg
- ½ cup Homemade Almond Paste (see recipe, page 93) *or* ½ of 8-ounce can almond paste
- 1 to 2 tablespoons milk
- ½ cup chopped light raisins

Heat and stir milk and butter just till warm (115° to 120°) and butter almost melts. Insert steel blade. Add *2 cups* flour, the yeast, sugar, and ½ teaspoon *salt.* Process with 2 or 3 on/off turns. Add *half* the milk mixture; process with 4 on/off turns. Add rest of milk mixture and egg; process with 4 on/off turns. Add remaining 1 cup flour; process with 4 on/off turns. Process about 15 seconds or till dough mounds around center. *Do not process more than 60 seconds.* (If dough seems sticky to the touch, add 1 to 2 tablespoons more flour; process with 1 or 2 on/off turns. Dough is soft.)

Place dough in lightly greased bowl. Cover; let rise in warm place till double (about 1 hour). Punch down; cover. Let rest 10 minutes. On floured surface roll dough to 18x12-inch rectangle.

Insert steel blade in work bowl; add Homemade Almond Paste and 1 tablespoon milk. Process with on/off turns till spreadable (add another tablespoon milk, if needed); spread over dough. Top with raisins. Roll up, jelly roll-style, starting at long side; seal.

Shape in ring on large greased baking sheet; seal ends. Divide into quarters, using kitchen shears to snip *almost* to center. Snip each quarter into thirds, making 12 sections. Gently pull sections apart; twist. Cover; let rise till double (about 45 minutes). Bake in 350° oven about 25 minutes. Makes 1 coffee cake.

Mexican Doughnuts

Also called Buñuelos, these have a slight anise flavor —

- ½ cup milk
- ¼ cup butter *or* margarine
- 1 tablespoon aniseed
- 1 teaspoon salt
- 2¾ cups all-purpose flour
- 1 teaspoon baking powder
- 2 eggs
  Cooking oil for deep-fat frying
- ½ cup sugar
- 1 teaspoon ground cinnamon

In small saucepan heat milk, butter or margarine, aniseed, and salt just till butter melts, stirring constantly.

Place steel blade in work bowl; add *2 cups* of the flour and the baking powder. Process with on/off turns till mixed. Add eggs and milk-butter mixture; process with on/off turns till flour disappears. Add remaining ¾ cup flour; process with on/off turns till flour disappears.

Turn out onto lightly floured surface. Shape dough into 20 small balls. Cover; let rest at least 10 minutes. Roll out 2 or 3 balls at a time to 4-inch circles. (Keep remaining balls of dough covered.)

Pour oil into 10-inch skillet to depth of about 1 inch. Heat to 375°, using a deep-fat frying thermometer to check temperature. (Or, check by dropping bread cube into hot oil; temperature is 375° if bread is lightly browned in 1 minute.) Fry 2 or 3 doughnuts at a time about 4 minutes or till golden brown, turning once. Drain doughnuts on paper toweling. Repeat rolling and frying rest of dough.

In paper or plastic bag combine sugar and cinnamon. Gently shake warm doughnuts, one at a time, in sugar mixture. Makes 20.

sauces

Tomato Sauce with Pepperoni

- 1 large onion, cut into 1-inch pieces
- ¼ cup lightly packed parsley (stems removed)
- ¼ cup lightly packed fresh basil (stems removed) *or* 2 teaspoons dried basil
- 2 cloves garlic, halved
- 6 large tomatoes, peeled and quartered (6 cups)
- 1 cup water
- 1 8-ounce can tomato sauce
- 2 teaspoons instant beef bouillon granules
- 1 teaspoon sugar
- ½ teaspoon salt
- 6 ounces pepperoni, casing removed
- 1 tablespoon cornstarch
  Hot cooked pasta

Place steel blade in work bowl; add onion, parsley, basil, and garlic. Process with on/off turns till finely chopped. Transfer to 3-quart saucepan. Reinsert steel blade in work bowl. Add *2 cups* of the tomatoes; process till smooth. Add to saucepan. Repeat with remaining tomatoes, processing 2 cups at a time. Add the water, tomato sauce, bouillon granules, sugar, and salt to saucepan. Bring to boiling; reduce heat and simmer for 45 minutes, stirring occasionally.

Rinse work bowl; insert slicing disk. Slice pepperoni; add to sauce. Blend cornstarch and 1 tablespoon cold *water*; add to sauce. Cook and stir about 5 minutes or till thickened and bubbly. Serve over pasta. Makes 6 servings.

Tomato Sauce with Pepperoni served on Green Noodles (see recipe, page 63)

Marinara Sauce

- 1 medium onion, cut up
- 1 medium carrot, cut up
- 1 clove garlic, halved
- 2 tablespoons cooking oil
- 3 16-ounce cans tomatoes
- 1½ teaspoons sugar
- ¾ teaspoon salt
- ½ teaspoon dried oregano, crushed

Place steel blade in work bowl; add onion and process with on/off turns till finely chopped. Remove from work bowl; set aside. Reinsert steel blade in work bowl; add carrot pieces and garlic. Process till finely chopped.

In 3-quart saucepan cook onion, carrot, and garlic in hot oil till tender. Reinsert steel blade in work bowl; add *1 can undrained* tomatoes. Process with on/off turns till coarsely chopped; add to saucepan. Repeat with remaining tomatoes, processing 1 can at a time. Add sugar, salt, oregano, and dash *pepper* to pan.

Boil gently, uncovered, about 1¼ hours or till desired consistency, stirring frequently toward end of cooking time. Serve hot with pasta, poultry, or meat. Makes 3½ cups.

Tartar Sauce

- ½ small onion, cut up
- 6 sprigs parsley (stems removed)
- 1 large dill *or* sweet pickle, cut into 1-inch pieces
- 1 hard-cooked egg, quartered
- 1 cup Homemade Mayonnaise (see recipe, page 55) *or* salad dressing

Place steel blade in work bowl; add first 4 ingredients. Process with on/off turns till chopped. Remove to bowl; stir in Homemade Mayonnaise or salad dressing. Cover; chill. Serve with fish. Makes 2 cups.

Eggplant-Tomato Sauce

- 8 ounces fresh mushrooms
- 1 16-ounce can tomatoes
- ½ medium eggplant, peeled and cut into 1-inch pieces (about 1¾ cups)
- 1 medium onion, cut into 1-inch pieces
- ½ stalk celery, cut into 1-inch pieces
- ¼ cup lightly packed parsley (stems removed)
- ¾ cup vegetable juice cocktail
- ¼ cup dry white wine
- 2 tablespoons olive oil *or* cooking oil
- 1 tablespoon worcestershire sauce
- 2 teaspoons sugar
- 1 teaspoon dried basil, crushed
- ½ teaspoon salt
- ¼ teaspoon dried thyme, crushed
- ¼ teaspoon dried oregano, crushed

Insert slicing disk in work bowl; slice mushrooms. Transfer to 3-quart saucepan. Place steel blade in work bowl; add *undrained* tomatoes. Process with on/off turns till chopped. Add to saucepan. Reinsert steel blade in work bowl; add eggplant. Process with on/off turns till finely chopped; add to saucepan.

Reinsert steel blade in work bowl. Add onion, celery, and parsley; process with on/off turns till finely chopped. Add to saucepan. Add vegetable juice cocktail, wine, oil, worcestershire, sugar, basil, salt, thyme, and oregano.

Bring to boiling; reduce heat. Simmer, uncovered, about 35 minutes or till thickened, stirring occasionally. Season to taste. Serve over pasta, fish, chicken, or hamburgers. If desired, pass grated parmesan cheese. Makes about 3½ cups.

Mornay Sauce

- 2 ounces gruyère cheese
- 2 tablespoons butter *or* margarine
- 2 tablespoons all-purpose flour
- ¼ teaspoon salt
  Dash white pepper
- 1½ cups milk
- 2 tablespoons dry white wine

Insert shredding disk in work bowl; shred cheese. In saucepan melt butter or margarine; blend in flour, salt, and pepper. Add milk all at once. Cook quickly, stirring constantly, till mixture thickens and bubbles. Add shredded cheese and wine; stir over low heat till cheese is melted. Serve with fish, poultry, or vegetables. Makes about 1¾ cups sauce.

Durango Sauce

- 1 15¾-ounce can barbecue beans
- 1 8-ounce can tomato sauce
- ⅓ cup bottled taco sauce
- 1 teaspoon worcestershire sauce

Place steel blade in work bowl; add beans, tomato sauce, taco sauce, and worcestershire sauce. Process till mixture is smooth. Use for basting pork chops, steaks, or hamburgers during last 5 minutes of barbecuing. Heat remaining sauce to pass, or add browned ground beef or sliced frankfurters and serve in buns. Makes about 2½ cups.

homemade horseradish

Be ready for a pungently strong aroma when uncovering the processed horseradish —

- 1 5-ounce horseradish root, peeled and cut into 1-inch pieces
- ¼ cup milk
- ¼ cup vinegar
- 1 tablespoon brown sugar
- 2 teaspoons prepared mustard
- 1 teaspoon salt
- ⅛ teaspoon pepper

Place steel blade in work bowl; add pieces of horseradish root. Process 1 to 2 minutes or till very finely chopped. Add milk, vinegar, brown sugar, mustard, salt, and pepper; process about 1 minute or till thoroughly blended. Turn into jar; cover and chill. Store in refrigerator. Makes about ¾ cup.

Horseradish Sauce

- ½ cup whipping cream
- 3 tablespoons Homemade Horseradish *or* prepared horseradish
- ⅛ teaspoon salt

Place steel blade in work bowl; add whipping cream. Process for 20 to 25 seconds or till thick. Add the Homemade Horseradish and salt; process with 1 or 2 on/off turns just till blended. Serve with meat. Makes ¾ cup.

Horseradish-Mustard Sauce: Prepare Horseradish Sauce as above *except* add 2 tablespoons *dijon-style mustard* with the Homemade Horseradish and salt.

Curry Sauce

This sauce is full of solids —

- 1 medium apple, cored and cut into 1-inch pieces
- 1 medium onion, cut into 1-inch pieces
- 1 small green pepper, halved
- 1 stalk celery
- 2 tablespoons butter *or* margarine
- 2 to 3 teaspoons curry powder
- 1 tablespoon all-purpose flour
- ¼ teaspoon salt
- 1 cup milk
- 1 teaspoon instant chicken bouillon granules
- ½ teaspoon worcestershire sauce

Place steel blade in work bowl. Add apple and onion pieces; process till coarsely chopped. Remove and set aside. Insert slicing disk; slice green pepper and celery.

In 1½-quart saucepan melt the butter or margarine; stir in the curry powder. Add the apple, onion, pepper, and celery. Cover and cook till tender but not brown. Stir in the flour and salt. Add milk, bouillon granules, and worcestershire sauce all at once. Cook over medium heat, stirring constantly, till mixture is thick and bubbly.

Serve with meat, fish, or poultry or spoon over rice or poached eggs. If desired, pass condiments such as chopped peanuts, shredded coconut (see tip, page 92), raisins, and chutney. Makes 2 cups.

French Onion Sauce

This variation of a favorite soup is shown below —

- ½ ounce parmesan cheese, cut up (2 tablespoons grated)
- 3 medium onions, halved
- 2 tablespoons butter *or* margarine
- 2 tablespoons cornstarch
- 1 10½-ounce can condensed beef broth
- ¼ teaspoon worcestershire sauce

 Place steel blade in work bowl. Add cut-up parmesan; process till finely chopped. Remove and set aside. Insert slicing disk in work bowl; slice the onions.

In a 2-quart saucepan cook the sliced onions in butter or margarine, covered, for 10 minutes. Uncover, cook 10 to 12 minutes more or till lightly browned, stirring occasionally. Stir in the cornstarch. Add the condensed beef broth and worcestershire all at once. Cook over medium heat, stirring constantly, till mixture thickens and bubbles. Cook 2 minutes more. Stir in parmesan; heat through.

To serve, spoon atop sliced roast beef on French bread or atop meat loaf, meatballs, or round steak. Makes about 2 cups.

Gazpacho Sauce

Shown above —

- 2 stalks celery, cut into 1-inch pieces
- ½ medium green pepper, cut into 1-inch pieces
- ½ small onion, cut into pieces
- ¾ cup tomato juice
- 1 tablespoon cooking oil
- 1 tablespoon wine vinegar
- 1 slice bread, torn into pieces
- 6 sprigs parsley (stems removed)
- ¼ teaspoon salt
  Dash garlic salt
  Dash pepper
  Few dashes bottled hot pepper sauce
- 1 medium tomato, peeled and quartered

Place steel blade in work bowl; add celery, green pepper, and onion. Process with on/off turns till coarsely chopped. Remove from work bowl; set aside.

Reinsert steel blade in work bowl; add tomato juice, oil, vinegar, bread, parsley, salt, garlic salt, pepper, and hot pepper sauce. Process till mixture is smooth. Add tomato and chopped vegetables to mixture in work bowl. Process with on/off turns just till tomato is coarsely chopped.

Transfer to bowl; cover and chill. Serve over tossed greens or with cooked meat or assorted cold cuts. Makes 2 cups.

Salsa

- 3 green onions, cut into 1-inch pieces
- 1 stalk celery, cut into 1-inch pieces
- ½ of a 4-ounce can green chili peppers, halved, rinsed, and seeded
- 2 tablespoons lightly packed fresh cilantro *or* parsley (stems removed)
- 1 large tomato, peeled and quartered
- 1½ teaspoons vinegar
- 1 teaspoon worcestershire sauce
- ¼ teaspoon garlic salt
- ¼ teaspoon dried oregano, crushed
- 2 drops bottled hot pepper sauce (optional)

Place steel blade in work bowl. Add onion and celery; process with on/off turns till finely chopped. Transfer to mixing bowl. Reinsert steel blade in work bowl; add chili peppers and cilantro or parsley. Process with on/off turns till finely chopped. Add to onion-celery mixture. Reinsert steel blade in work bowl. Add tomato; process with on/off turns till coarsely chopped. Add to onion-celery mixture; add vinegar, worcestershire sauce, garlic salt, oregano, and hot pepper sauce. Mix lightly. Cover and chill overnight. Serve with beef roasts or steaks. Makes about 1¾ cups.

Sweet and Pungent Sauce

Instead of using fresh pineapple and tomatoes, you can substitute one 8¼-ounce can crushed pineapple and one 8-ounce can tomatoes —

- ½ small pineapple, peeled, cored, and cut up
- 2 tablespoons brown sugar
- 4 teaspoons cornstarch
- 1 small green pepper, cut up
- ½ small onion, cut up
- 2 medium tomatoes, halved
- 2 tablespoons vinegar
- 1 tablespoon soy sauce

Place steel blade in work bowl; add pineapple. Process with on/off turns till finely chopped (should yield 1 cup). Pour fresh or canned pineapple into sieve or colander to drain, reserving ⅓ cup juice. In 1-quart saucepan combine reserved pineapple juice, brown sugar, and cornstarch.

Place steel blade in work bowl; add green pepper and onion. Process with on/off turns till coarsely chopped. Leave pepper and onion in work bowl; add fresh or undrained canned tomatoes. Process with 2 or 3 on/off turns just till tomatoes are coarsely chopped. Add to saucepan; stir in vinegar and soy sauce.

Cook and stir till thickened and bubbly. Stir in drained pineapple; heat through. Serve with meat or poultry. Cover and refrigerate any remaining. Makes about 2½ cups.

thickening sauces

You can use cooked vegetables to thicken sauces and gravies instead of cornstarch or flour. When making a pot roast or stew, take out some of the cooked vegetables (include a few pieces of cooked potato) and process till smooth. Add enough of the meat juices through the feed tube to make the gravy or sauce of the desired consistency.

Green Mole

- 1 12-ounce can tomatillos (green Spanish tomatoes), rinsed and drained
- 1 4-ounce can green chili peppers, rinsed, seeded, and cut up
- ½ medium onion, cut up
- ⅓ cup chicken broth
- ¼ cup firmly packed fresh cilantro or parsley (stems removed)
- ¼ cup walnuts or almonds
- ¼ teaspoon salt
  Dash pepper

Place steel blade in work bowl; add all ingredients. Process about 1 minute or till nearly smooth. Transfer to 1-quart saucepan; heat through. Serve with meat or poultry. Makes 1¾ cups.

Avocado-Mushroom Sauce

Shown below —

- ½ small onion, cut up
- ½ cup fresh mushrooms
- 1 tablespoon butter or margarine
- 1 tablespoon all-purpose flour
- ¼ teaspoon salt
- ½ cup milk
- 1 ripe medium avocado, seeded, peeled, and cut into 1-inch pieces
- ½ cup dairy sour cream

Place steel blade in work bowl; add onion. Process with on/off turns till finely chopped. Add mushrooms; process with on/off turns till coarsely chopped.

In 1½-quart saucepan cook onion-mushroom mixture in butter or margarine till tender. Stir in flour and salt. Add milk all at once. Cook and stir over medium heat till thick and bubbly. Remove from heat.

Place steel blade in work bowl; add avocado. Process till smooth. Stir avocado and sour cream into sauce; heat through, but *do not boil.* Serve at once. Spoon over open-faced bacon-lettuce-and-tomato or chicken sandwiches, poached eggs, baked potatoes, or omelets. *Or,* serve as hot dip with chips, crisp vegetables, or boiled shrimp. Makes 1½ cups sauce.

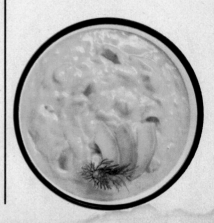

Quick Applesauce

4 medium cooking apples,
   peeled, cored, and
   quartered
¼ cup sugar
¼ cup water
1 teaspoon lemon juice

Place steel blade in work bowl; add apples. Process till coarsely chopped. Add sugar, water, and lemon juice. Process with on/off turns till well mixed and desired smoothness. Spoon into serving dishes; sprinkle with ground cinnamon, if desired. Serve at once. Makes about 2 cups.

Brandy Hard Sauce

1 cup butter, chilled and cut into
   pieces
1 16-ounce package powdered
   sugar
2 tablespoons whipping cream
2 tablespoons brandy
1 teaspoon vanilla

Place steel blade in work bowl; add butter. Process till soft and fluffy. With machine running add *1 cup* of the unsifted powdered sugar through feed tube, ¼ *cup* at a time. Add *1 tablespoon* of the cream; stop and scrape bowl.

Add remaining powdered sugar, remaining 1 tablespoon cream, brandy, and vanilla; process till smooth, stopping to scrape bowl if needed. Spoon into covered container and chill. Serve atop plum pudding, baked apples, or warm fruit pies. May be refrigerated up to 6 weeks or frozen up to 6 months. Makes 2½ cups.

Peppermint Sauce

10 hard peppermint candies
1 7-ounce jar marshmallow
   creme
2 tablespoons milk

Place steel blade in work bowl; add peppermint candies. Process till finely crushed (should have ¼ cup). Transfer to 1½-quart saucepan. Add marshmallow creme and milk. Heat and stir till blended. Add a little additional milk, if needed, to make desired consistency. Serve warm over ice cream. Makes about 1¾ cups.

Pineapple Sauce

This may be frozen in freezer containers, if desired —

1 large pineapple, peeled,
   cored and cut up (6 cups)
2 1-inch strips lemon peel (cut
   with vegetable peeler)
1½ cups sugar
½ cup light corn syrup
3 tablespoons lemon juice

Place steel blade in work bowl; add *2 cups* of pineapple. Process with on/off turns till finely chopped; transfer to 3-quart saucepan. Repeat with remaining pineapple, 2 cups at a time; add lemon peel to last batch (should have total of 4 cups chopped fruit). Add sugar and corn syrup to pineapple in pan. Bring to full boil. Reduce heat; boil gently, uncovered, 20 to 25 minutes or till almost desired consistency (mixture thickens as it cools). Stir frequently to prevent sticking. Stir in lemon juice.

Pour hot sauce into hot clean canning jars, leaving ½-inch headspace. Prepare lids according to manufacturer's directions; wipe rims and adjust lids. Process in boiling water bath for 10 minutes (start timing when water returns to boiling). Makes 4 or 5 half-pints.

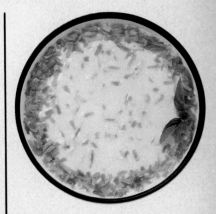

Coconut Dessert Sauce
Shown above —

1 fresh coconut
   Milk
1 4-serving-size package *instant*
   vanilla pudding mix
½ teaspoon vanilla

Open coconut (refer to tip on page 92). Drain and reserve coconut liquid; shell and peel coconut. Insert shredding disk in work bowl; shred coconut. Remove from bowl; measure *1 cup* of the coconut and spread in a single layer in 15x10x1-inch baking pan. Toast in 325° oven 15 to 20 minutes or till lightly browned, stirring occasionally. Set aside. Freeze remaining coconut for another use. Measure coconut liquid; add milk to make 3¼ cups.

Place steel blade in work bowl; add *2 cups* of the coconut liquid-milk mixture, the pudding mix, and vanilla. Process 20 seconds or till blended. Transfer to storage container; stir in the remaining coconut liquid-milk mixture. Cover; chill.

Just before serving, stir in ½ *cup* of the toasted coconut. Spoon atop fruit or cake, sprinkling the remaining toasted coconut atop each serving. Makes about 3 cups.

jams & relishes

Three-Fruit Marmalade

A blend of cantaloupe, pineapple, and orange —

- 3 cantaloupes, halved (6 pounds total)
- 1 pineapple, peeled and cored (2½ pounds)
- 2 oranges
- 5 cups sugar
- 3 tablespoons lemon juice

⊘ Remove and discard melon seeds; scoop pulp into large bowl. Cut pineapple into 1-inch pieces; add to melon.

Using vegetable peeler, cut thin layer of peel from oranges; cut peel into 1-inch pieces and add to fruit. Squeeze juice from oranges (should have ⅔ cup); set aside.

Place steel blade in work bowl. Add 2 cups of the fruit mixture; process with on/off turns till finely chopped. Transfer to large kettle or 8-quart Dutch oven. Repeat to make a total of 8 cups finely chopped fruit, processing 2 cups at a time. Stir in the reserved ⅔ cup orange juice, the sugar, and the lemon juice.

Bring fruit mixture to full rolling boil. Boil hard, uncovered, 40 to 45 minutes or till syrup sheets off a metal spoon. Stir frequently to prevent scorching, especially during the last 10 minutes. Fill jars and process as directed in tip on page 82. Makes 5 or 6 half-pints.

Spiced Apple Butter
Apricot-Raspberry Jam
Three-Fruit Marmalade

Spiced Apple Butter

- 5 pounds tart cooking apples, peeled, cored, and quartered (about 12 cups)
- 3 cups apple cider
- 2½ cups sugar
- 1½ teaspoons ground cinnamon
- ¼ teaspoon ground cloves

⊘ In large saucepan bring apples and cider to boiling; reduce heat. Simmer, covered, 20 to 25 minutes or till apples are tender. Place steel blade in work bowl; add 2 cups of the apples. Process till smooth; transfer to 13x9x2-inch baking dish. Repeat with remaining apples, processing 2 cups at a time. Stir sugar, cinnamon, and cloves into apples.

Bake in 300° oven for 2 to 2½ hours or till thick when spooned; stir every half hour to prevent edges from overcooking. Fill jars and process as directed in tip on page 82. Makes 7 half-pints.

Cherry Conserve

- 2 pounds dark sweet cherries, stemmed and pitted (5 cups)
- 1 small lemon
- 2 cups sugar
- ½ cup slivered almonds
- ⅓ cup flaked coconut

⊘ Place steel blade in work bowl; add half of the cherries. With a vegetable peeler, cut four 1-inch strips of lemon peel; add to work bowl. Process with on/off turns till finely chopped; transfer to 4-quart Dutch oven. Repeat with remaining cherries. Squeeze lemon; measure 2 tablespoons juice and add to cherries. Add sugar; bring to full boil. Boil, uncovered, for 12 minutes; stir occasionally. Stir in almonds and coconut; remove from heat. Skim off foam. Fill jars and process as directed in tip on page 82. Makes 3 or 4 half-pints.

Apricot-Raspberry Jam

- 2 pounds fresh apricots, pitted
- ½ pint fresh raspberries
- 1 1¾-ounce package powdered fruit pectin
- 2 tablespoons lemon juice
- 7 cups sugar

⊘ Place steel blade in work bowl; add half of the apricots. Process with on/off turns till chopped; transfer to 5-quart Dutch oven. Repeat with remaining apricots, plus raspberries (should have about 4½ cups total chopped fruit). Stir in pectin and lemon juice. Bring to hard boil, stirring constantly. Stir in sugar. Bring to hard boil; stir constantly. Boil vigorously, uncovered, 1 minute. Remove from heat; skim off foam. Stir and skim for 5 minutes. Fill jars and process as directed in tip on page 82. Makes 7 half-pints.

Carrot Marmalade

- 6 medium carrots, cut up
- 2 medium tart cooking apples
- 1 medium pear
- 6 1-inch strips lime peel (cut with vegetable peeler)
- 2 cups sugar
- 1 cup honey
- ⅓ cup lime juice

⊘ Place steel blade in work bowl; add 3 carrots. Process till finely chopped; transfer to 4-quart Dutch oven. Repeat with rest of carrots (for total of 2 cups finely chopped). Reinsert steel blade. Peel and core apples and pear. Cut into 1-inch pieces; add to work bowl. Add lime peel; process with on/off turns till finely chopped. Add to carrots. Stir in sugar, honey, and lime juice. Bring to boil; reduce heat. Boil gently 20 minutes or till thickened; stir often. Fill jars; process as directed in tip on page 82. Makes 3 or 4 half-pints.

Apricot-Honey Butter

1½ pounds fresh apricots, pitted
    and quartered
1½ cups sugar
¾   cup honey
3   tablespoons frozen orange
    juice concentrate, thawed

Cook apricots, covered, in ¼ cup *water* for 10 to 12 minutes. Place steel blade in work bowl; add *2 cups* of the apricots. Process till nearly smooth. Remove; repeat with remaining apricots. Measure 3 cups puree into a 4-quart Dutch oven. Stir in sugar and honey. Bring to full boil; reduce heat. Boil gently 15 to 20 minutes or till mixture cooks down to 3 cups; stir constantly. Stir in juice concentrate. Fill jars and process as directed in tip, right. Makes 3 half-pints.

Apple-Grape Spread

3½ pounds tart cooking apples,
    peeled, cored, and
    quartered
2   cups grape juice
7   cups sugar
1   tablespoon lemon juice
1   3-ounce foil pouch (½ of
    6-ounce package) liquid
    fruit pectin
½   teaspoon ground cinnamon

In 4- to 5-quart Dutch oven combine apples and grape juice. Simmer, covered, 15 to 20 minutes or till very soft. Place steel blade in work bowl; add *2 cups* apple mixture. Process till nearly smooth; remove to bowl. Repeat with remaining, processing 2 cups at a time. Measure 5 cups puree into Dutch oven. Stir in sugar and lemon juice. Bring to full rolling boil; boil vigorously 1 minute. Remove from heat; stir in pectin and cinnamon. Stir and skim off foam for 5 minutes. Fill jars; process as directed in tip, right. Makes 8 half-pints.

canning jams

Jam-type products are generally fruit-based and preserved by sugar, using natural pectin, plus commercial pectin if necessary, to form a gel. When using commercial pectin, be sure to follow the recipe directions exactly. Do not use more or less than the amount of sugar called for or the product won't gel as it should.

Do not try to double jelly or jam recipes. Having a larger amount of fruit mixture will change the cooking time needed for the gel. If you want to make more, simply repeat the recipe and make consecutive batches.

Water bath processing is a relatively new step that's been added to the home preparation of jam-type products. Research shows that heat processing for 5 to 15 minutes does not alter these products but does destroy molds that may be present on the top surface. Also, the heat processing helps seal the jars.

Fill the water bath canner with 4 to 5 inches of water. Cover and heat. Fill the hot clean canning jars, leaving ¼-inch headspace. Prepare lids according to manufacturer's directions. Wipe jar rim; adjust lid. Place on rack in water bath canner; add boiling water to cover tops of jars. Return water to boiling. Process 15 minutes (start timing when water boils).

Autumn Chutney

2   cloves garlic, quartered
2   1-inch strips candied ginger
2   whole canned green chili
    peppers, halved seeded,
    and rinsed
2   medium papayas, seeded,
    peeled, and cut into 1-inch
    pieces
4   medium tart cooking apples,
    peeled, cored, and cut into
    1-inch pieces
1   medium green pepper, cut into
    1-inch pieces
½   medium onion, cut into 1-inch
    pieces
1   cup packed brown sugar
¾   cup vinegar
½   cup raisins
½   cup water
3   tablespoons lime juice
1   teaspoon salt
½   cup slivered almonds

Place steel blade in work bowl; add garlic and candied ginger. Process till very finely chopped. Add chili peppers; process with on/off turns till chopped. Transfer to 5-quart kettle.

Reinsert steel blade in work bowl; add *1 cup* of the papaya pieces. Process with on/off turns till chopped. Remove and repeat for total of 4 cups chopped papaya; add to kettle. Reinsert steel blade in work bowl; add *1 cup* of the apple pieces. Process with on/off turns till chopped. Remove and repeat for total of 2 cups chopped apple; add to kettle.

Reinsert steel blade in work bowl; add the green pepper and onion. Process till chopped; add to fruit mixture. Stir in brown sugar, vinegar, raisins, water, lime juice, and salt. Simmer, covered, for 30 minutes, stirring frequently. Stir in almonds. Cook, uncovered 30 minutes more, stirring often to prevent sticking. Cool. Store, covered, in refrigerator or freeze in moisture-vaporproof containers. Makes 6 cups.

Peach Chutney

1½ cups sugar
1 cup vinegar
½ cup lemon juice
½ cup currant jelly
1 tablespoon salt
1 teaspoon ground ginger
¼ teaspoon cayenne
4 pounds peaches, pitted
2 medium green peppers
2 medium sweet red peppers
1 cup light raisins

In 5-quart Dutch oven, mix first 7 ingredients. Bring to boil; keep warm. Place steel blade in work bowl. Peel peaches. Cut up peaches and peppers; add 1 cup to work bowl. Process with on/off turns till chopped; stir into vinegar mixture. Repeat with rest of peaches and peppers, 1 cup at a time. Stir in raisins. Bring to boil. Boil gently 25 to 30 minutes or till thick; stir occasionally. Fill jars. Process as directed in tip on page 84. Makes 8 half-pints.

Pineapple Chutney

1 medium pineapple, peeled, cored, and cut up
1 8-ounce package pitted whole dates, halved
1 1-inch strip candied ginger
¼ cup raisins
2 tablespoons sugar
2 tablespoons vinegar
¼ teaspoon ground cinnamon

Place steel blade in work bowl; add 2 cups pineapple. Process with on/off turns till finely chopped. Transfer to 2-quart saucepan; repeat with rest of pineapple, plus dates and ginger, processing 2 cups at a time. Stir rest of ingredients and ½ cup *water* into fruit mixture. Bring just to boil; reduce heat. Simmer 10 minutes or till slightly thickened; stir occasionally. Serve warm or chilled; refrigerate remaining. Makes 3½ cups.

Mexican Relish

1 small clove garlic
1 4-ounce can green chili peppers, rinsed and seeded
½ large green pepper, cut up
½ large onion, cut up
2 pounds tomatoes, peeled
2 teaspoons chili powder
1 teaspoon salt
½ teaspoon ground cumin

Place steel blade in work bowl; add garlic and chili peppers. Process till finely chopped. Add pepper and onion. Process till coarsely chopped; transfer to 2-quart saucepan. Reinsert steel blade. Quarter tomatoes into work bowl. Process till coarsely chopped; drain. Measure 2½ cups pulp; add to pan. Stir in seasonings. Simmer 30 minutes. Serve warm or chilled; refrigerate remaining. Makes 2½ cups.

Sicilian Relish

2 medium green peppers
2 stalks celery
2 medium carrots
½ cup pitted ripe olives
⅓ cup pimiento-stuffed olives
½ cup cooking oil
½ cup white vinegar
1 teaspoon salt
½ teaspoon dried oregano
⅛ teaspoon pepper
Dash garlic powder

Cut up peppers and celery. Place steel blade in work bowl; add 2 cups pepper mixture. Process with on/off turns till chopped; remove. Repeat with rest of pepper mixture, 2 cups at a time. Insert shredding disk; shred carrots. Insert slicing disk; slice olives. Add to vegetables. Insert steel blade; add oil, vinegar, and seasonings. Process till blended; stir into vegetables. Cover; chill 2 to 3 days. Drain. Makes 3½ cups.

Zucchini Relish

Turmeric tints the relish yellow and gives it a flavor similar to corn relish —

4 to 4½ pounds zucchini, cut into 1-inch pieces
2 medium onions, cut into 1-inch pieces
1 medium sweet red pepper, cut into 1-inch pieces
2 tablespoons salt
1½ cups sugar
1 cup vinegar
1 cup water
2 teaspoons celery seed
1 teaspoon ground nutmeg
1 teaspoon ground turmeric (optional)
⅛ teaspoon pepper

Place steel blade in work bowl; add 2 cups of the zucchini. Process with on/off turns till coarsely chopped; transfer to large bowl. Repeat with remaining zucchini, plus onions and red pepper, processing 2 cups at a time.
Sprinkle salt over vegetables. Cover and refrigerate overnight. Rinse in cold water; drain well. Transfer vegetables to 4- to 5-quart kettle or Dutch oven. Stir in the sugar, vinegar, water, celery seed, nutmeg, turmeric, and pepper.
Bring to boiling; reduce heat. Boil gently, covered, for 10 minutes, stirring often. Fill jars with hot relish and process as directed in tip on page 84. Makes 4 pints.

Corn Relish

5 to 7 ears fresh corn
½ small head cabbage, cored and cut into 1-inch pieces
3 stalks celery, cut into 1-inch pieces
2 medium onions, cut into 1-inch pieces
1 medium cucumber, seeded and cut into 1-inch pieces
1 medium green pepper, cut into 1-inch pieces
1 medium sweet red pepper, cut into 1-inch pieces
1 cup vinegar
⅓ cup water
⅓ cup honey
3 tablespoons sugar
1 tablespoon salt
1 teaspoon celery seed
1 teaspoon dry mustard
1 teaspoon ground turmeric

Husk corn. Cook in boiling water 5 minutes (start timing when water returns to boil); plunge into cold water. Drain; cut corn from cobs (do not scrape cobs). Measure 3 cups corn; place in 4- to 5-quart kettle or Dutch oven.

Place steel blade in work bowl; add *half* of the cabbage. Process with on/off turns till chopped; remove. Repeat with remaining cabbage. Measure 2 cups cabbage; add to corn. Reinsert steel blade in work bowl; add celery. Process till chopped; measure 1 cup and add to corn. Repeat with onion, then cucumber, adding 1 cup of each to corn. Repeat with green pepper, then red pepper, adding ¾ cup of each to corn.

Combine vinegar, water, honey, sugar, salt, celery seed, dry mustard, and turmeric; stir into vegetable mixture. Bring to boiling; boil gently, uncovered for 15 minutes, stirring occasionally. Cool. Store, covered, in refrigerator or freeze in moisture-vaporproof containers. Makes about 6 cups.

canning relishes

Relishes are heat processed to destroy spoilage-causing organisms and any molds that may be present on the top surface.

Fill water bath canner with 4 to 5 inches water; cover and heat. Fill hot clean canning jars with hot relish, leaving ½-inch headspace. Prepare lids according to manufacturer's directions. Wipe jar rim; adjust lid. Place on rack in water bath canner; add boiling water to cover tops of jars. Return water to boiling. Process 10 minutes (start timing when water boils).

Shredded Carrot Relish

1 small onion, cut up
1 small green pepper, cut up
8 ounces carrots
⅓ cup sugar
⅓ cup vinegar
¼ cup water
½ teaspoon salt
8 whole cloves

Place steel blade in work bowl; add onion and green pepper. Process with on/off turns till finely chopped. Transfer to mixing bowl; set aside. Insert shredding disk; shred carrots. Add to onion and pepper.

In saucepan combine remaining ingredients; bring to boiling. Reduce heat; simmer, covered, 10 minutes. Pour through strainer over vegetables; discard whole cloves. Stir vegetables to mix well. Cover; chill overnight. Makes 1½ cups.

Tomato-Apple Relish

This relish can be frozen in pint or half-pint freezer containers, also —

3 medium green peppers, cut into 1-inch pieces (2 cups)
3 medium sweet red peppers, cut into 1-inch pieces (2 cups)
4 large onions, quartered (4 cups)
10 to 12 medium tart cooking apples, cored and quartered (10 cups)
10 medium tomatoes, cored and quartered (8 cups)
2½ cups sugar
2½ cups vinegar
2 tablespoons salt
1 teaspoon ground allspice

Place steel blade in work bowl; add 2 cups of the peppers. Process till chopped; transfer to 10-quart kettle or Dutch oven. Repeat with remaining peppers, onions, apples, and then tomatoes, processing 2 cups at a time.

Stir in the sugar, vinegar, salt, and allspice. Bring to boiling, stirring occasionally. Reduce heat and boil gently, uncovered, about 1¼ hours or till desired consistency, stirring occasionally.

Fill jars and process as directed in tip, left. Makes 6 pints.

Tomato-Apple Relish
Shredded Carrot Relish
Corn Relish

desserts

Cheesecake Supreme

¾ cup all-purpose flour
6 tablespoons cold butter, cut into pieces
3 tablespoons sugar
4 1-inch strips lemon peel (cut with vegetable peeler)
1 egg yolk
¼ teaspoon vanilla

For crust, place steel blade in work bowl; add ¾ cup flour, butter, 3 tablespoons sugar, and 4 strips lemon peel. Process till peel is finely chopped and mixture is crumbly. Add 1 egg yolk and ¼ teaspoon vanilla; process just till mixture forms a ball. Pat ⅓ of the dough on bottom of 8-inch spring-form pan (sides removed).

Bake in 400° oven about 7 minutes or till golden; cool. Butter sides of pan; attach to bottom. Pat remaining dough on sides of pan to height of 1¾ inches; set aside.

3 8-ounce packages cream cheese, quartered
1 cup sugar
¼ cup milk
2 tablespoons all-purpose flour
2 1-inch strips lemon peel (cut with vegetable peeler)
¼ teaspoon salt
¼ teaspoon vanilla
2 eggs
1 egg yolk

For filling, place steel blade in work bowl (no need to wash work bowl after preparing crust). Add cream cheese, 1 cup sugar, milk, 2 tablespoons flour, 2 strips lemon peel, salt, and ¼ teaspoon vanilla. Process till mixture is creamy, scraping bowl as needed. With machine running add eggs and 1 egg yolk through feed tube. Process till smooth, scraping bowl occasionally. Turn into crust-lined pan.

Bake in 350° oven for 50 to 60 minutes or till center appears set. Remove from oven; cool 15 minutes in pan. Loosen sides of cheesecake from pan with spatula. Cool 30 minutes more. Remove sides of pan. Cool 2 hours more before adding glaze.

1 cup fresh pineapple cut into chunks (½ of 1 medium) or ¾ cup canned crushed pineapple
¼ cup water
3 to 4 tablespoons sugar
1 tablespoon cornstarch

For glaze, place steel blade in work bowl; add fresh pineapple chunks. Process with on/off turns till chopped. Transfer to 1-quart saucepan; add water. (Or, combine canned crushed pineapple and water.) Bring to boil over medium-high heat. Boil gently, uncovered, for 2 minutes.

Thoroughly stir together 3 to 4 tablespoons sugar (taste pineapple for sweetness) and cornstarch; stir into the boiling fruit. Cook and stir about 1 minute or till thickened. Cool to room temperature. Spoon over cooled cheesecake; chill at least 2 hours before serving. Makes 12 servings.

Homemade Mincemeat

1 pound beef neck or ½ pound beef stew meat
3 medium oranges
1 medium lemon
2½ cups sugar
2 pounds tart cooking apples, peeled, cored, and cut into 1-inch pieces
8 ounces beef suet, cut into 1-inch cubes
4½ cups raisins
2½ cups dried currants
½ cup diced candied fruits and peels
1½ teaspoons salt
½ teaspoon ground nutmeg
¼ teaspoon ground mace

In saucepan cover beef neck or stew meat with water. Bring to boiling; reduce heat. Simmer, covered, 2 to 3 hours. Cool; drain.

Meanwhile, use vegetable peeler to cut three 1-inch strips of peel from one orange and two 1-inch strips from lemon. Squeeze oranges, reserving ¼ cup juice. Squeeze lemon, reserving ¼ cup juice. Place steel blade in work bowl; add peels and ½ cup sugar. Process 20 seconds or till chopped. Transfer to 4-quart Dutch oven.

Remove meat from neck bones; cut meat into 1-inch pieces. Mix with apples and suet. Reinsert steel blade in work bowl; add 2 cups of the meat mixture. Process with on/off turns till coarsely chopped; remove to Dutch oven. Repeat with remaining meat mixture, processing 2 cups at a time.

Stir in raisins, currants, candied fruits and peels, salt, nutmeg, mace, the remaining 2 cups sugar, reserved orange and lemon juices, and 2½ cups water. Simmer, covered, 1 hour; cool. Cover and refrigerate or freeze in moisture-vaporproof containers. Makes 12 cups (fills three 9-inch pies).

Cheesecake Supreme

Letterbanket

These also are called Dutch Letters —

½ cup Homemade Almond Paste
   (see recipe, page 93) *or* ½ of
   8-ounce can almond paste
1 egg yolk
2 tablespoons sugar
1½ cups all-purpose flour
¼ teaspoon salt
¾ cup butter *or* margarine,
   chilled and cut into pieces
¼ cup ice cold water
1 egg white
2 teaspoons water

Place steel blade in work bowl; crumble Homemade Almond Paste into work bowl. Add egg yolk and sugar; process till thoroughly mixed. Remove; cover and chill.

Return steel blade to work bowl; add flour and salt. Process with 3 on/off turns just to mix. Add butter; process with on/off turns till mixture resembles coarse crumbs. With machine running add ice water quickly through feed tube; process just till dough is moistened (over-processing will make dough tough).

Remove dough and use hands to shape it into a ball. Cover; let stand 30 minutes. Divide dough in half. On lightly floured surface roll one half to an 8-inch square; cut into four 8x2-inch strips. Repeat to make four more strips.

Roll about 1½ tablespoons of the chilled almond paste mixture into a rope about 7½ inches long; repeat to make 8 ropes. Place one rope in center of each strip of dough. Fold dough over rope, completely sealing sides and ends (moisten edges of dough, if necessary, to ensure a complete seal).

Shape into desired letters on ungreased cookie sheets. Combine the egg white and 2 teaspoons water; brush on letters. Bake in 375° oven about 25 minutes or till golden brown. Cool. Makes 8 letters.

Deluxe Fruit Ice Cream

2 cups fresh *or* frozen
   unsweetened raspberries
1 pound fresh peaches, pitted
   and peeled, *or* 2 cups frozen
   unsweetened peaches
1 ripe banana, cut up
2 cups sugar
1 cup orange juice
½ cup lemon juice
3 cups milk
2 cups whipping cream

Thaw frozen fruits. Place steel blade in work bowl; add fruits. Process till smooth, scraping bowl as necessary; transfer to large bowl. Reinsert steel blade; add sugar, orange juice, lemon juice, and ¼ teaspoon *salt*. Process till sugar is dissolved. Add to fruit mixture; pour into 4-quart ice cream freezer container. Add milk and whipping cream; stir well. Freeze according to manufacturer's directions. Makes 3½ quarts.

Frozen Cherry Macaroon Dessert

6 coconut macaroon cookies,
   broken
¼ cup maraschino cherries,
   drained
1 quart chocolate ice cream

Place steel blade in work bowl; add cookies. Process till finely crushed; remove. Reinsert steel blade; add cherries. Process with on/off turns till finely chopped; add to crumbs. Reinsert steel blade; add *one-fourth* of the ice cream. Process till softened. Continue processing ice cream, adding one-fourth at a time. Add crumb mixture. Process just till blended.

Spoon into paper bake cup-lined muffin pans *or* into one 8x4x2-inch loaf pan. Cover; freeze 4 hours or overnight. Makes 8 or 9 servings.

Watermelon Ice

½ medium watermelon
1½ cups sugar
⅓ cup lemon juice
   Dash salt
1 envelope unflavored gelatin
⅓ cup water

Scoop out watermelon pulp, discarding seeds. Place steel blade in work bowl; add about 2 *cups* of the watermelon pulp. Process till smooth; measure and remove to large bowl.

Repeat with enough of the remaining watermelon to make total of 6 cups puree. Stir in the sugar, lemon juice, and salt, mixing well.

In small saucepan soften gelatin in water; stir over low heat till gelatin is dissolved. Add gelatin to melon mixture; blend thoroughly. Pour mixture into 13x9x2-inch pan; cover and freeze till partially frozen.

Place steel blade in work bowl; add *half* of the partially frozen mixture. Process with on/off turns till machine runs smoothly, then let machine run till ice is smooth, fluffy, and lighter in color. Return to pan. Repeat with remaining partially frozen mixture. Cover and freeze firm. Makes about 8 cups ice.

Cantaloupe Ice: Halve 2 medium *cantaloupe* and discard seeds. Scoop out pulp. Process 2 *cups* cantaloupe pulp as directed above for watermelon. Repeat, processing 2 cups at a time, to make total of 6 cups puree. Continue as directed above.

Deluxe Fruit Ice Cream
Letterbanket

Pumpkin Cake Roll

- 1 cup walnuts
- 3 eggs
- 1 cup granulated sugar
- ⅔ cup canned pumpkin
- 1 teaspoon lemon juice
- ¾ cup all-purpose flour
- 2 teaspoons ground cinnamon
- 1 teaspoon baking powder
- 1 teaspoon ground ginger
- ½ teaspoon salt
- ½ teaspoon ground nutmeg
- 2 3-ounce packages cream cheese, halved
- ¼ cup butter, cut into pieces
- ½ teaspoon vanilla
- 1 cup powdered sugar

Place steel blade in work bowl. Add nuts; process till chopped. Remove from bowl; set aside. Reinsert steel blade; add eggs and process 35 to 40 seconds or till lemon-colored. With machine running add granulated sugar; process till thoroughly combined and slightly thickened. Add the pumpkin and lemon juice; process with on/off turns just till mixed.

Stir together the flour, cinnamon, baking powder, ginger, salt, and nutmeg; add to work bowl. Process with 2 or 3 on/off turns just till flour disappears. *Do not overmix.* Spread batter in greased and floured 15x10x1-inch baking pan. Sprinkle with the chopped walnuts.

Bake in 375° oven for 15 minutes. Turn out onto towel sprinkled with a little powdered sugar. Starting at narrow end, roll up cake and towel together, nuts on outside of roll. Cool, seam side down, on rack.

Meanwhile, place steel blade in clean work bowl; add cream cheese, butter, and vanilla. Process till mixture is smooth. Add 1 cup powdered sugar; process till smooth. Unroll cooled cake; spread with cream cheese mixture. Reroll; chill at least 2 hours. Slice to serve. Makes 10 servings.

Carrot-Pineapple Cake

Shown on page 4 —

- 2 or 3 carrots
- ¾ cup fresh pineapple cut into 1-inch pieces *or* ½ cup canned crushed pineapple
- 1½ cups all-purpose flour
- 1 cup sugar
- 1 teaspoon baking powder
- 1 teaspoon baking soda
- 1 teaspoon ground cinnamon
- ½ teaspoon salt
- ⅔ cup cooking oil
- 2 eggs
- 1 teaspoon vanilla
  Cream Cheese Frosting

Insert shredding disk in work bowl; shred carrots to make 1 cup. Set aside. Place steel blade in work bowl; add fresh pineapple. Process with on/off turns till finely chopped; measure ½ cup pineapple. Set aside.

Rinse work bowl; dry. Reinsert steel blade. Add flour, sugar, baking powder, soda, cinnamon, and salt; process with 3 or 4 on/off turns. Add the 1 cup shredded carrot, ½ cup fresh or canned pineapple, oil, eggs, and vanilla. Process with on/off turns just till all is moistened, scraping bowl as needed; let machine run 20 seconds more. Pour batter into greased and lightly floured 9x9x2-inch baking pan. Bake in 350° oven 35 minutes. Cool. Frost with Cream Cheese Frosting.

Cream Cheese Frosting: Place steel blade in work bowl. Add 2½ cups *powdered sugar;* one 3-ounce package *cream cheese,* quartered; ¼ cup *butter or margarine,* cut into pieces; 1 teaspoon *vanilla;* and dash *salt.* Process till smooth and creamy, scraping bowl as needed. (If mixture is too stiff, add 1 teaspoon *milk;* process till smooth.) Add ½ cup *pecans;* process with on/off turns just till nuts are coarsely chopped. Spread over cooled cake.

Cranberry Cheese Pie

- 1 14-ounce can *sweetened condensed* milk
- 2 3-ounce packages cream cheese, quartered
- ⅓ cup lemon juice
- ½ teaspoon vanilla
  Graham Cracker Crust
- 1 16-ounce can whole cranberry sauce
  Unsweetened whipped cream

Place steel blade in work bowl. Add the sweetened condensed milk, cream cheese, lemon juice, and vanilla. Process till smooth; turn into chilled Graham Cracker Crust. Carefully spoon cranberry sauce atop cheese mixture in pie shell; stir gently to marble.

Freeze several hours or overnight till firm. Let pie stand about 10 minutes at room temperature before serving. Garnish with unsweetened whipped cream. Slice pie and serve immediately.

Graham Cracker Crust

- 18 graham cracker squares
- ¼ cup sugar
- 6 tablespoons butter, melted

Place steel blade in work bowl; break crackers into bowl. Add sugar. Process till very finely crushed. With machine running add melted butter through feed tube; process till well mixed. Press mixture firmly and evenly onto bottom and sides of a 9-inch pie plate. Chill 45 minutes or till firm. *Or,* bake in 375° oven for 6 to 9 minutes or till edges are just brown; cool. Makes one 9-inch crust.

Plain Pastry

For Lard Pastry, substitute ⅔ cup cold lard, cut into pieces, for the shortening; use ⅓ cup ice cold water —

- 2 **cups all-purpose flour**
- ⅔ **cup shortening**
- 1 **teaspoon salt**
- ¼ **cup ice cold water**

Place steel blade in work bowl; add flour, shortening, and salt Process with on/off turns till most of mixture resembles cornmeal but a few larger-size pieces remain. Have ice cold water in a cup. With machine running, quickly add ice cold water through feed tube; stop processor as soon as all water is added. Scrape down sides. Process with 2 on/off turns (mixture may not all be moistened). Remove dough and shape into 2 equal balls. (If dough is soft, chill 30 minutes before rolling.) Makes two 9-inch single-crust pastries or one 9-inch double-crust pastry.

For single crust: Turn dough out on lightly floured surface. Roll to circle about 12 inches in diameter; transfer to 9-inch pie plate. Trim dough to ½ inch beyond edge of pie plate; fold excess under and flute edge. For baked crust, prick bottom and sides all over with a fork. Bake in 450° oven for 10 to 12 minutes.

For double crust: Roll one ball of dough out and fit into pie plate as for single crust; *do not prick*. Trim dough even with edge of pie plate. Roll out second ball of dough; cut slits for escape of steam. Place atop filling in pie shell; trim as for single crust. Fold excess under bottom crust and flute. Bake as directed in recipe.

using fresh coconut

To open a fresh coconut, use a sharp instrument, such as an ice pick, to pierce the three eyes of the coconut. Drain the coconut milk; reserve milk, if desired. Tap the coconut all over with a hammer until the shell cracks and falls off or can be pulled off. Use a vegetable peeler or sharp knife to remove the brown covering from the white meat. Store fresh coconut in covered container in refrigerator for up to 3 days *or* freeze in airtight container.

To shred coconut: Insert shredding disk in work bowl. Cut white meat into pieces to fit feed tube; shred.

To slice coconut: Insert slicing disk in work bowl. Cut white meat into pieces to fit feed tube; slice.

Candied Coconut Chips

- 2½ **cups water**
- 1½ **cups granulated sugar**
- 1½ **cups sliced fresh coconut (see tip, above)**
- ⅔ **cup granulated sugar *or* colored sugar**

Bring water and the 1½ cups sugar to boiling, stirring occasionally. Boil, uncovered, 25 to 30 minutes or till mixture resembles corn syrup and measures 1 cup. Remove from heat; stir in coconut slices. Using slotted spoon lift out a few pieces at a time; quickly roll in the ⅔ cup sugar. Let dry, lightly covered, on cheesecloth-covered rack for 1 to 2 days. Makes 2 cups.

Nut Butter-Coconut Bars

- 1 **cup sugar**
- ½ **cup Nut Butter (see recipe, page 51)**
- 6 **tablespoons butter**
- 2 **eggs**
- 1 **teaspoon vanilla**
- 1 **cup whole wheat flour**
- 1 **teaspoon baking powder**
- ¼ **teaspoon salt**
- ¾ **cup shredded coconut (see tip, left)**

Place steel blade in work bowl; add first 3 ingredients. Process till creamy. Add eggs and vanilla; process with 2 or 3 on/off turns till blended. Add mixture of flour, baking powder, and salt; add coconut. Process with 2 or 3 on/off turns just till flour disappears. Spread in greased 11x7½x2-inch baking pan. Bake in 375° oven for 25 to 30 minutes. Cool; cut. Makes 2 dozen.

Thumbprint Cookies

- ¾ **cup butter *or* margarine**
- ½ **cup sugar**
- 2 **eggs**
- 1½ **teaspoons vanilla**
- 2 **cups all-purpose flour**
- 1½ **teaspoons baking powder**
- ½ **cup Nut Butter (see recipe, page 51) *or* jam**

Place steel blade in work bowl; add butter and sugar. Process till creamy. Add eggs and vanilla; process till blended. Add mixture of flour, baking powder, and ¼ teaspoon *salt*; process with 2 or 3 on/off turns just till flour disappears. Cover; chill at least 3 hours. Shape into 48 balls; place 2 inches apart on greased cookie sheets. Moisten thumb; make indentation in each ball. Press in ½ *teaspoon* Nut Butter or jam. Bake in 375° oven 10 to 12 minutes. Makes 4 dozen.

Almond Bars

- 2 cups all-purpose flour
- 1 cup cold butter *or* margarine, cut into 8 chunks
- ¼ cup ice cold water
- 1 cup Homemade Almond Paste *or* 1 8-ounce can almond paste
- 1 cup sugar
- 2 eggs
- ½ teaspoon vanilla

🌀 Place steel blade in work bowl; add flour and butter. Process with on/off turns till mixture resembles cornmeal. Have ice cold water in cup. With machine running pour ice cold water all at once through feed tube. Process about 20 seconds or till most of mixture is crumbly (some dry areas may still be visible).

Remove dough and use hands to form it into a ball; divide in half. Wrap in waxed paper; chill several hours or overnight.

To make filling, reinsert steel blade in work bowl; crumble Homemade Almond Paste into work bowl. Add sugar, eggs, and vanilla; process till smooth.

To prepare bars, let chilled dough stand at room temperature about 30 minutes or till just soft enough to handle. On lightly floured surface roll *half* the dough to 14x10-inch rectangle. Place in bottom and ½ inch up the sides of a 13x9x2-inch baking dish. Spread filling over dough to within ½ inch of pastry edge. Roll out remaining dough to 14x10-inch rectangle; place atop filling. Press edges to seal. Bake in 400° oven 30 to 35 minutes. Cool; cut into bars. Makes 4 dozen.

homemade almond paste

If you can't find whole blanched almonds, follow the directions below for blanching —

- 1 cup whole blanched almonds (6 ounces) *or* 1⅓ cups slivered almonds
- 1⅓ cups sifted powdered sugar
- 2 tablespoons water
- ½ teaspoon almond extract (optional)

🌀 Place almonds in a single layer on baking sheet. Heat in 300° oven for 10 minutes; do not brown. Remove; cool 5 minutes.

Place steel blade in work bowl; add almonds. Process about 1 minute or till ground. Add powdered sugar, water, and extract (if desired for a stronger almond flavor). Process about 15 seconds or till mixture forms a ball. Use immediately or wrap and store in refrigerator or freezer. Makes about 1 cup.

How to blanch whole almonds: Place almonds in saucepan; cover with water. Bring to boiling; drain. Skins should slip off easily when almond is pressed between thumb and forefinger.

Chocomint Dessert

- 1 13-ounce can evaporated milk
- 1 6-ounce package lime-flavored gelatin
- 1 cup boiling water
- ⅓ cup green crème de menthe
- 1 8½-ounce package (38) chocolate wafers
- 1 roll (12) white peppermint hard candies
- 6 tablespoons butter *or* margarine, cut into pieces
- 1 8-ounce package cream cheese, quartered
- 1 cup sugar

🌀 Pour evaporated milk into 8x8x2-inch pan; cover and freeze till crystals form around edges. Dissolve gelatin in boiling water; stir in crème de menthe. Let cool 20 minutes.

Place steel blade in work bowl; add chocolate wafers and peppermint candies. Process till finely crushed; add butter. Process till well mixed. Press ⅔ of the crumbs over bottom of 13x9x2-inch baking pan.

Wipe out work bowl; reinsert steel blade. Add cream cheese and sugar; process till smooth. With machine running add gelatin through feed tube; process till well mixed.

Using electric mixer whip partially frozen evaporated milk to soft peaks; fold in cheese mixture. Pour atop crust. Sprinkle with remaining crumbs. Chill 6 hours or overnight. Makes 16 servings.

index

tips & information